GARTH BROOKS

THE ANTHOLOGY | PART THREE

Produced by

MELCHER MEDIA

124 West 13th Street
New York, NY 10011
www.melcher.com

10 9 8 7 6 5 4 3 2 1

Manufactured in China
Library of Congress Control Number: 2018938110

Standard First Edition:
ISBN 978-1-59591-039-4

GARTH BROOKS
THE ANTHOLOGY | PART THREE

LIVE

WRITTEN BY
GARTH BROOKS
WITH WARREN ZANES

 MELCHER MEDIA    PEARL RECORDS

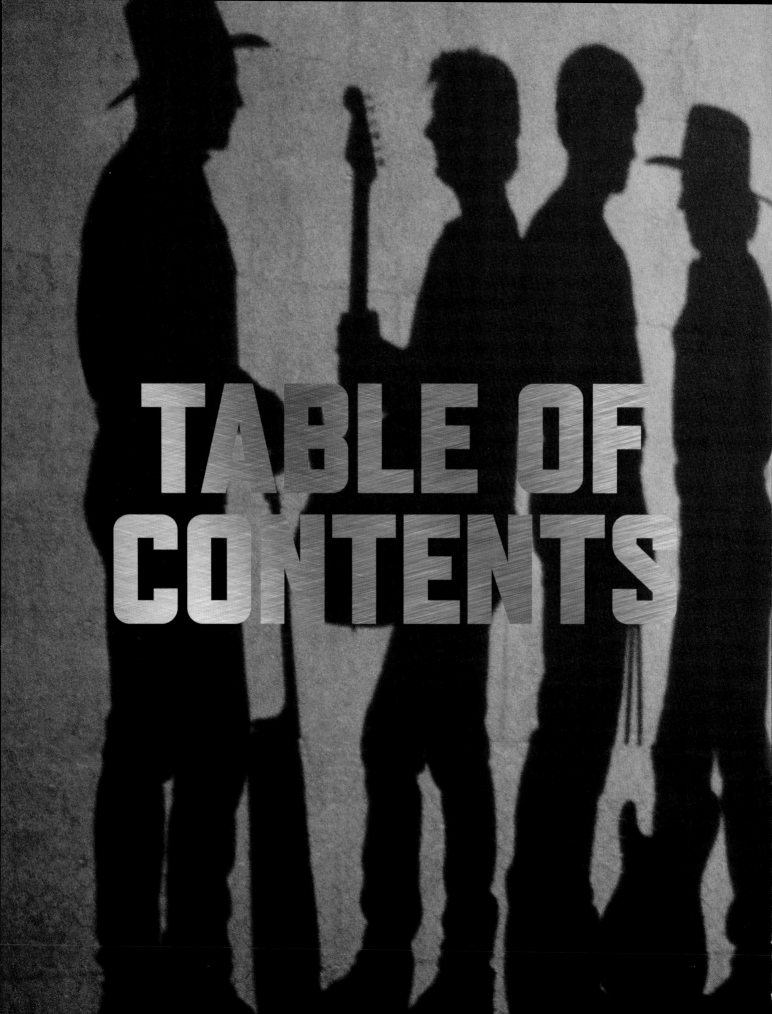

TABLE OF CONTENTS

① CENTRAL PARK

AUGUST 7, 1997

For the first time, ever, HBO announced a country concert in Central Park.

No one had ever thought of New York City as the home of country music. By the time you drove through the Lincoln Tunnel or crossed the George Washington Bridge into Manhattan, you couldn't find a radio station playing country. That belonged to another America. Or so it seemed as July turned to August in the summer of 1997.

Since its founding, America had established deep roots in farming, as a place where lives were lived close to the soil. But the nation's identity had been splitting apart since the Industrial Revolution. The rural and the urban were forcibly separated by the changes that would shape 20th century life, and the two Americas, it seemed, had lost contact with one another. In 1985, the *New York Times* declared country music dead. No one in Manhattan, the Bronx, or Brooklyn stood up to dispute the claim.

When Garth Brooks came to New York City to play Central Park, however, something happened that suggested maybe, just maybe, those two Americas weren't completely lost to one another. The concert was a long shot. In the past, Central Park was reserved for the biggest pop acts in the world . . . but they were always acts that had some connection to New York City.

The weather was perfect and though it had rained the night before, that did not discourage the hundreds who slept on the sidewalk just outside the park in order to be the first let in the following day. Those hundreds would turn to thousands and those thousands would turn to hundreds of thousands.

At 3 p.m. that day, Parks Services had opened up the overflow viewing areas and were seriously considering shutting down Fifth avenue . . . two hours later, Fifth Avenue was shut down.

And as the sun was going down over Manhattan on August 7, something was becoming clear: Country music did make sense there. And those two Americas, seemingly out of touch with one another, were still connected. In fact, the biggest concert in the park's history was about to take place. It was a unifying moment, a symbol of what music could do to bridge two worlds that had lost contact. And in this case, country music was doing it. Planting roots in the middle of Manhattan.

To bring it to New York City in this way . . .
IT FELT LIKE A VICTORY FOR ALL COUNTRY MUSIC! -g

BOB DOYLE: I've known Garth a long time. Since before he started recording. And I'll tell you, as Garth's manager, I could see that he has always had a real connection to his audience. Heart to heart. He's always had it, had it when he came to town. A real entertainer. But bringing it to Central Park was meaningful to us all. And, really, I think it was meaningful to country music.

TRACY GREENWOOD: Building up to it, it was scary for me because . . . well . . . it's New York! I'm from there. So I was working as a kind of assistant on the road and the part I remember most was thinking about the New York attitude I grew up with. I was hoping they weren't just going to eat him for lunch.

JIMMY MATTINGLY: Well, the thing about that gig was that we hoped it was gonna be big. But we didn't know for sure, partly because they didn't sell tickets. It was free. But it was also New York. I played fiddle, and I knew there weren't a lot of fiddlers up that way.

G: *(laughs)* The guy who's probably best to talk to about this would be Pat Quigley. He's the one that set it all up. Damn, it's one of the greatest promotion stories ever, how he pulled that off.

PAT QUIGLEY: I think there are different kinds of people in life. There are people who don't want to take a risk and people who *do* want to take a risk. And I love to take a risk, and that means you might fail. I'd say Garth's the same. Around the time before Central Park, I'd read a biography of Aristotle Onassis, had just finished it. Now, when Onassis was young, he had nothing to speak of to work with, to build his fortune. This is after World War II, and America was booming and needed oil from the Middle East. Onassis goes to the Middle East and says, "I control all the Greek ships, so give me the contracts for the oil." He gets all the contracts, then he goes back to Greece and says, "I control all the oil, give me the ships." He didn't have any ships or any oil, and he became a zillionaire. I looked at his example and said, *You don't need all the pieces in place, you just have to take a risk.* So I made a phone call to Giuliani's office, and they gave me to a guy named Henry Stern, who was the Parks Commissioner of New York City.

It was scary for me because . . . well . . .
IT'S NEW YORK!
- TRACY GREENWOOD

G: The parks guy, Henry Stern, was the sweetest guy on the planet. I can still see his face.

PAT QUIGLEY: Henry Stern is an interesting guy for a variety of reasons, but the first thing you notice with him is that he's got a golden retriever, and when you pet the dog Henry reaches in his pocket, takes out a little counter, and goes *click*. Then he explains that his dog is going for the Guinness World Record for having the most people pet him. I was like number 126,540. Henry walked this dog in New York City. It's easy to get people to pet your dog in New York City, especially a golden retriever. You pet the dog, he clicks the counter. That's Henry Stern. I said, "Henry it's an election year, and I want to bring Garth Brooks to Central Park." He goes, "Unbelievable, let's do it."

G: So Pat's looking at New York City, not known to be a country music mecca and wants to take this to HBO, who's never done a country music special.

PAT QUIGLEY: I knew that New York City is not just Manhattan. When you're in the Hamptons or, say, upstate, you can listen to different music than you listen to in Manhattan. So in my mind it was about the entire metropolitan area. But I also believed that, culturally, country music can't be afraid to go into major markets. My thought was that if the people show up at all it will be a success in New York, and that as an antenna New York is the most important media market in the world. If we put on the same concert in Lexington, Kentucky, HBO wouldn't have taken it. The risk was the important thing for everybody, I think. HBO had to take the chance on something unexpected, and if it worked it would be a success for country, for Garth and for HBO.

So I had Central Park and HBO, but I didn't have Garth because I hadn't even told him I was going to New York. I called him. I remember, I was standing on the corner of Sixth Avenue and 42nd Street in New York City. I said, "I've got Central Park and I've got HBO. I need you to take this show." I'll never forget, clear as a bell he said, "You're the boss." He got it immediately. He said, "I'll do it." And it was over.

THE NORTH MEADOW WAS SEVEN FOOTBALL FIELDS IN LENGTH AND FIVE FOOTBALL FIELDS WIDE, AND THEN THERE WAS ANOTHER AREA THAT WAS ABOUT NINE FOOTBALL FIELDS IN LENGTH.
– JON SMALL

G: Next thing we find out is that they're re-seeding the Great Lawn, the space in Central Park where Simon and Garfunkel played. That's the spot, the place we thought we'd be playing. But they have another location for us, they say, the North Meadow. That sounds nice, right? The North Meadow. Well, what they didn't tell me was that the North Meadow was five times the size of the Great Lawn. And it wasn't set up for shows. When I went to New York and walked out to the space we were going to be playing, I about swallowed my tongue. I'm sitting there going, *No fucking way we're gonna fill this up.* It's impossible. I'm thinking, *How the hell did I let myself get talked into this?* If ten people show up in this North Meadow, how's that going to look on HBO? Now, I'd already worked with Jon Small on a few videos, and this was when he came in as producer. Whatever happens, *whatever* happens, this has to look good. Ten people or not. I was leaning on Jon.

JON SMALL: One of the cool things with Garth was that he'd tell people, "This is the guy I want you to work with." So I was really forced on everybody. But I still had to pass the test with HBO. I remember walking down the hall at HBO in New York, getting ready for my interview with them, thinking, *I better be good.* They started asking me all these questions, and I finally said to them, "You're asking the wrong questions." They said, "What do you mean we're asking the wrong questions?" I said, "You're not asking me what I'm bringing to the table as the producer." So Nancy Geller at HBO goes, "Well, what are you bringing to the table as the producer?" I said, "I'm bringing Garth, I'll show you." I picked up the phone and dialed Garth, and he picks up. I go, "Garth, I'm with

HBO." Garth says, "Great, how's it going?" I go, "Great, I'll call you later." I hung up and said to them, "See that, that's how quick I get to Garth." That was it, the interview was over. I went back to my hotel room, and Garth calls me asking how it went. I tell him I think it went great. He goes, "Well, it must have gone great because they just called me to say you're the guy to do it."

PAT QUIGLEY: A lot of people thought there would be a bunch of mobile homes and trailers and fiddles laying around on the ground in Central Park.

JON SMALL: Yes, there were doubters. They didn't know who would be coming to this show. I remember we were setting up and a bicyclist rode by and yelled, "Nobody's coming!" The North Meadow was seven football fields in length and five football fields wide, and then there was another area that was about nine football fields in length. I was going to install screens everywhere so people, wherever they looked, could see that show. But when we started there was nothing there. There was no infrastructure whatsoever, nothing. It took ten days to build the stage. Half the people didn't think anybody was going to show up, the other half believed that this would draw a crowd. But, either way, it was a huge task for us to get this done.

LANNY LANDERS: I remember living on the bus at Central Park. Our hotels were across the river somewhere way off, not in Manhattan. I was a rigger, and the calls for riggers were early, earlier than lighting or sound calls, so I just stayed on the bus in Central Park. It was great, just being there, getting up and running in the morning. It was nice and quiet. We just kind of camped out there.

JON SMALL: What happens first is that all the steel gets loaded in. The steel is what supports the stage. Then it's the wood for the decks, and we build everything that the musicians stand on. That stage? I think it was 480 feet wide, gigantic, and 90 feet deep. So it was really a big thing to build, and it was August, very hot. I had to have showers put out there for the crew.

G: When we get to rehearsal the night before the show, you know, we're out there rehearsing and at the end of every song, there's applause. We couldn't figure it out.

JOHN KINSCH: I was handling guitars then, I think. Garth and the band would get finished with a song, and you'd hear the echo from the music die down and, way off in the distance, you'd hear people cheering, clapping. It was kind of weird.

GARTH LIVE FROM CENTRAL PARK

FREE CONCERT THURSDAY, 8 PM AUGUST 7, 1997

Presented by

City of New York/Parks & Recreation
Rudolph W. Giuliani, Mayor
Henry J. Stern, Commissioner

G: You can't figure it out until you look under the trees and down Fifth Avenue, all the way down, and . . . *they're just lined up.* They've got their sleeping bags. And you're going, *Are you kidding me?!*

MIKE PALMER: We were blocking for the camera the night before, and it was raining, so it kept getting pushed back. The park police wouldn't let us on the stage. Finally, it dries up, and we were able to get on the stage. But it was getting late, so I had to play my drums quietly with brushes, just to mimic through songs so they could get an idea of where everyone was going to be. Then Garth decides, "Hey, for the intro, let's come out to Art Garfunkel's 'A Heart in New York.'" We'd go from that, he tells us, straight into "Rodeo." But they're two different tempos. I was already kind of nervous, you know. But he wants to add this, last minute, tells me just to speed the tempo up as we get into "Rodeo."

JON SMALL: Billy Joel came in the day before to rehearse the two songs that he was going to do, "New York State of Mind" and "Ain't Going Down ('Til the Sun Comes Up)." So Billy comes in to rehearsal, sits down at the piano, starts noodling around, and the band is like in awe watching Billy play. So Garth says, "Hey, Billy, give us some jukebox!" Billy looks at me like, *What does that mean?* I say, "He wants you to play some of your songs." Billy starts rolling into some of the songs, but he's always in a rush, so pretty quickly he gets to working on "New York State of Mind." They all start playing it, and all of a sudden Billy stops the band and goes, "No, no guys, I want you to play sloppy, play it like you're The Rolling Stones, you know like it's a dark bar, late at night." They start playing it again, and Billy stops them again. He goes to Mike Palmer, the drummer, and says, "You're just not getting it, it needs to be sloppier." Mike says to Billy, "Well, we're all nervous because we've never played with this big of a star before." Garth goes, "Well, thanks, Mike." *(laughs)* That was such a candid moment, but it was so . . . that's how they felt. They'd never played such a big show, with a big star before, so they were kind of feeling their nerves.

G: I went back to the hotel that night just drained. We had a room next to Central Park, overlooking where we'd be playing the next day. By the following morning, man, I haven't slept much at all. I've got all the shades pulled. But you can hear helicopters. It's New York City, even at that time in the morning, and I'm just laying there. Sandy's going, "Hey, I want to turn on the news or something, I want to see what's happening." I said, "No, please don't, please let's just try to sleep as long as we can." I didn't want to face what I was getting ready to face, because I knew nobody was going to show up.

PAT QUIGLEY: The word of mouth was really growing. Living in New York, I just knew that everybody was coming.

G: So we manage to get back to sleep for a bit. But around noon, maybe one, Sandy just says she can't do it anymore and has to get up. She goes, "I've got to find out what's going on." And she heads into the next room. Ten minutes later she's back. And she's crying. I remember looking at her going, "Oh no, there's nobody there, is there?" She says, "Garth, they've already opened up the overflow. They think there's over half a million already." . . . You don't forget a moment like that. Ever.

MIKE PALMER: Jimmy and I had gone out during the day and kind of walked through the park. We didn't realize that beyond this first crowd we saw there was another field full of people. And even then it was just people, people as far as you could see. And we weren't even close to showtime. From that point, it was hard not to think about how it was going to feel once we were actually *up there*. This thing was getting bigger than anyone thought it could be.

JON SMALL: One of the first things you learn when you do this kind of work is that you can't put the artist in a bad light. And the only thing I knew Garth absolutely wanted was for the audience to be as close to the front of the stage as possible. The problem was that the police department insisted there be a barricade fifty feet out from the stage. That would leave a big, dead space in front of the stage.

I look at him and say, "You are telling me we have 850,000 people?" He goes, "NO, I'M SAYING 90 MINUTES AGO YOU HAD 850,000." -g

G: Barricades? I guess I understand what they're for. But if there's a physical distance between the artist and the people that allow that person to *be* an artist, that's a problem. I don't like that.

JON SMALL: I'm getting nowhere with these people. It was kind of like who has the biggest balls, is it the New York City Police Department or Jon Small. *(laughs)* I'm just a producer. I'm nothing to them. So I go, "Who's really in charge here?" The policeman I'm talking to says, "I am." Then I hear another voice say, "No, I am." I look, and it's the fire department, that's who was really in charge on this issue. I start saying, "Look, this is what we're going to do: I'm going to build an area in the front of the stage that will hold 1,500 people and . . ." but before I can go on, that captain cuts me off and says, "No, you're not." And I said, "Wait, let me finish . . . and those 1,500 people will be firemen's families, policemen's families, EMS families, and we'll sprinkle it with some special Garth

HEY GARTH....
YOU HAVE PLENTY OF
" Friends In Low Places "
N.Y. & LONG ISLAND
♥'s You

fans, like 500 Garth fans." They all looked at me like *(pause)* "Okay, that's a good idea." *(laughs)* And that's exactly how we did it.

PAT QUIGLEY: I certainly would have felt it was a victory with 250,000 people in the audience, because we don't do things to set a record. So if the crowd was that size, Garth would have been really happy, we all would have been happy.

G: It's time . . . We are walking to the stage and one of the park guys that's running things comes up beside me and hands me a piece of paper. I go, "What's this?" He says, "That was the count about 90 minutes ago." I open it up and it says 850,000. I look at him and say, "You are telling me we have 850,000 people?" He goes, "No, I'm saying 90 minutes ago you had 850,000."

My face is white, and
I DON'T HAVE A CLUE
what is getting ready to happen. -g

JON SMALL: You really had to see it.

G: One of the production team asked me if I wanted to take a look. I said no. I said, "No, it's the first time I'll be on live TV, and I want the first time I see that audience to be the first time they see me."

JIMMY MATTINGLY: Talking about adrenaline, my God. It's all you can do, man, just to calm down and be ready to play.

G: There are photographs of me underneath the stage. Henry Diltz took them. Brad Wathne, the stage manager, is right beside me at that moment, looking at me, and he goes—and he'd never asked this before—"You okay, boss?" I go, "Yeah, why?" He says, "You look . . . whiter than usual." In that shot, I look like a ghost. My face is white, and I don't have a clue what is getting ready to happen. But I get in that little elevator, and we get up there and go into Art Garfunkel's "A Heart in New York," then into "Rodeo" and, damn, here we go. That crowd is there, and I'm still looking at my boots, all the way, now I'm flush with the stage. I still haven't looked up. I'd played to crowds of 17,000 people in arenas, and that was big to me. I finally look up. Estimates are between 900,000 and 1.2 million people. And it's just people as far as you can see.

"The weather is perfect. If I could have had a word with God and said, I'd like this kind of weather . . . well, God was going, 'You think that's good, watch this.' The sound is perfect, and here it begins. And it's just . . . I don't know . . . I don't even know how to explain it. It never let up, it never waned. It only got more sincere when the darkness took over.

IT GOT MORE LOVING. IT WAS JUST ONE OF THE THINGS WHERE EVERYBODY SHOWED UP AND NOBODY LEFT."

- g

JON SMALL: Nobody knew that Billy Joel was going to be there. There were rumors, but there was no formal announcement. We staged it so that as Garth is singing "Shameless," a Billy Joel song, Billy actually walked out onstage, towards the end of the song, and Garth kind of turns towards Billy and does a double take. The crowd went crazy. Garth says something like, "I been out here an hour and a half busting my ass and you come out and in 10 seconds you get a bigger applause than what I get. *(laughing)"* It was great.

G: It's such a beautiful night. Billy Joel comes out and the place gets so loud. It's his hometown, and I'm such a Billy Joel fan. The crowd worshipped him, and I was right with them. He sat down at that big-ass grand piano and started "New York State of Mind." This place goes apeshit, and here comes Jim Horn to do the sax solo on it. It's a night made in heaven for me. I'm sitting there just . . . I'm getting to be a fan.

PAT QUIGLEY: It was all about New York and all about Garth. Two things I really care about found each other and had this magic moment.

IT'S SUCH A BEAUTIFUL NIGHT.
Billy Joel comes out and the place gets so loud.
It's his hometown, and I'm such a Billy Joel fan. - g

TRISHA YEARWOOD: I remember watching it on HBO, because I wanted to see and support my friend. I remember when he came out, seeing this look on his face. I thought, *He's overwhelmed by the people there.* But it's going to be okay. From where I was sitting, I just knew immediately that this was going to be good, was going to be really good.

G: We've had this night like no other, then you're getting ready to go back out for the encore and the only song you have left is "Much Too Young (To Feel This Damn Old)," which these people aren't going to know. It's New York, and it's your first single. But, my God, that fiddle starts and those people go up and you go, *no way . . .* They start to sing with you. So me and James Garver, the guitar player, we are out on this T that went out from the stage on the right, a T that shot out, I'm going to say, 20-30 yards, and at the end two or three of you could stand there side by side. It's going to the steel and fiddle solo, so we're not singing, we're not doing much while the others solo, so we just drop our mics down and kind of start talking while we're playing. I tell James my hometown had like 17,000 people when we moved there. He says his town was even smaller. I said to him, "Have you ever seen . . ." He goes, "Nope, never seen anything like this." And we just got to stare out at the people. I can't explain what it's like to see that many people in one area. It was beautiful.

31

a way to end that night. The director was a guy named Marty Callner, and he just got one of those perfect shots and the dream ending to all of this. You know, the cowboys came to New York and it worked. So the crown jewel for us and our career is probably Central Park. All the stereotypes of what country music is, what the country music fan was, it all went out the window. Over any pop or rock thing that ever happened in Central Park . . . it rang the bell for country music. It rang the bell for that country music audience. The country music audience was articulate, they were kind. They were attentive. They were respectful. I think in that moment everything everybody ever thought about what the country music audience was . . . got smashed. Whether it lasted 30 seconds after the show was over, I don't know. But in that moment, the whole world was watching the country music audience at its best.

TRISHA YEARWOOD: I feel like at every turn when you think Garth is at the top of his game, something happens to elevate it higher. I think Central Park was one of those things. It took a career that was huge and took it to the next level. It was great for country music. It elevated country music's game when New York said, "We love this Garth Brooks." It just took country music to places it wasn't normally seen or where you wouldn't expect to see it.

G: For a guy that has always felt like he wasn't the darling of the country music community, I was so glad when, after that show, we kept hearing three words, "We did it." When I heard those words, "We did it, as the country music community, together," it probably made me more proud than anything I ever got to do on my own. To think back, all the way back to my beginnings, to my first time getting onstage, and to think we brought this music here, to Central Park, and had that night . . . what a long way we'd come.

"I can't explain what it's like
to see that many people in one area.
IT WAS BEAUTIFUL."
- g

PAT QUIGLEY: What I knew was that Garth transcended country music. Garth is an entertainer. People in Central Park stood up for three hours. Because they realized they are seeing history, someone really, really special. And I think Garth had the heart and the intellect to take on the responsibility of delivering that performance.

THE CROWN JEWEL
for us and our career is probably
CENTRAL PARK. -g

G: You're at the end, but you still have the ace in the hole left, because it's the last song of the night and you're going to start out singing . . . "A long, long time ago." You start singing "American Pie" and you're going to sing the first verse and the chorus of what might be the most known song in music history, and you're going to say, "Ladies and gentlemen, please welcome . . ." but before you can finish, well, it's done. Here comes the man himself. All in black. It's Don McClean, and, damn, he looks great. Don gets out there, and there's just a little bit of breeze so he looks kind of like . . . it's perfect. He just starts in. But now he's sung this song so much that his melody is a little different than what we grew up on. And when he gets to the chorus, he really slows it down. And I'm sitting there going, *oh, crap.* Because we didn't *rehearse* it! It's "American Pie." I'm going, *oh, crap, I don't know how to get this thing back up to the speed that I'm used to doing it.*

But damn if it didn't work out really well, because he had it so slow and the people were so pulled in by it . . . then here comes that chorus. You can imagine . . . everybody knows the song. You have to be born on some other planet to not know this song! What

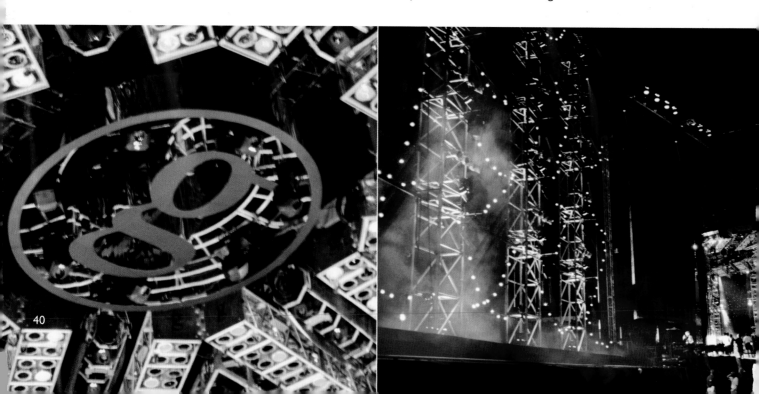

"CENTRAL PARK RANG THE BELL FOR COUNTRY MUSIC."

- g

"For a guy that has always felt like he wasn't the darling of the country music community, I was so glad when, after that show, **WE KEPT HEARING THREE WORDS, WE DID IT.**"

- g

August in New York had always been known to test the soul of man. Temperatures could reach 100 degrees plus humidity. But on that August 7, 1997, some mercy was shown. The high had been a pleasant eighty-one degrees, the sun was shining, and the winds were at six miles per hour. The city streets were buzzing as always. From New York radios blared the city's soundtrack: Notorious B.I.G., The Backstreet Boys, Mariah Carey, Puff Daddy. If there was a man on a tractor somewhere, you couldn't see him from Broadway and 43rd. But by the time of day's end, country music had given its heart to Manhattan . . . and been loved right back. As *The New York Times* reported, "The concert's biggest audience was in New York, where it scored a 51.7 rating in HBO homes, by far the biggest number ever for any HBO program." *Rolling Stone* magazine crowned it, "The highest rated music special of 1997. Estimated crowd counts started at over 900,000 and went as high as 1.2 million people."

It was a turning point in country's long history. While no one could stop the digital revolution that was well underway, with the internet changing lives across the globe, country arrived as a reminder that, no matter those changes, in music it would always come down to the singer and the song. And that was good news.

BEGINNINGS

2

-1985

In 1972, the Country Music Awards were held at the historic Ryman Auditorium in Nashville and hosted by Glen Campbell.

It had been a year in which many among the legends of country scored number one hits, including Merle Haggard, Tammy Wynette, Buck Owens, and Loretta Lynn, who was crowned Entertainer of the Year by the CMAs.

Garth Brooks turned ten years old and was living in Yukon, Oklahoma, when Loretta Lynn accepted that award. He would go on to receive the same award a record six times. He didn't know that then, nor did he know that he was one answer to the question: Where is country music heading? But he did know he heard something deep when Merle Haggard played on the family stereo. Same with George Jones and James Taylor. He didn't distinguish by genre, just by what he liked and didn't like. If it moved him, it became a part of his life. And along the way, many miles down that road, his wide range of musical favorites would shape the future of his music.

EVERY PERFORMER
starts doing what they do long before there's a stage in the room. - g

G: I didn't think of the stage as anything other than the point of focus in the room. That's what the stage is. It's your pulpit, and you're either seen from it or you're watching it. I don't know if there *is* another view. But performing wasn't anything that was new or odd to our family. We were raised with it.

Remember, my mom was a performer. One weekend out of every month she would perform at the Moose Lodge. My sister, well she was the most talented in the entire family, a blues guitarist, singer, songwriter, performer. So I grew up watching all these people perform. We had what we called talent night at the house, you know, like every Friday night or something. Each kid would get up and do something, and Dad played guitar and Mom sang.

TRISHA YEARWOOD: I think it was something that we had in common. He's the youngest of six, I'm the youngest of two. And we're both sort of the hams in our families. In some ways, you're not ever going to have tougher critics than your family. They're not going to laugh unless you've earned it. It makes you try even harder. I think that getting up in front of people is something we do because we did that as little kids. Our families got us started. I know Garth's dad played guitar, and his mom sang, so it was already in the living room. With my family it was the same.

"If you grow up in a house with music and performance around you,

IT'S NOT QUITE AS BIG A STEP TO GET TO THE STAGE."

- g

G: If you grow up in a house with music and performance around you, it's not quite as big a step to get to the stage. But, remember, as I got older, I also had my brother Kelly kind of showing me some things. There were six kids, and Kelly was a year and a half older. Mom and Dad kind of stuck Kelly with me, like whatever Kelly was going to do, he had to take his little brother with him. When Kelly could get a job at 16 and drive to it, little brother got a job at 14, and Kelly took him to work. And when Kelly wanted to go to a concert? He had to take his little brother with him. Not necessarily a good deal for Kelly, but for me he was kind of the hero. The first concert I went to with him was Styx, and . . . *holy cow*. We were probably three or four rows up from the roof, but, *oh my gosh*, it's cool! The next concert he took me to was Kansas. The rock shows left such an impression.

TY ENGLAND: Garth had an understanding for what to do in front of an audience, like some kind of understanding that was just . . . *in him*. I was still trying to get around my guitar, let alone get around a stage, but I really think he was eighty percent the performer he is today before he even got to Nashville.

My dad sent me to college to KEEP ME FROM PLAYING MUSIC. -g

G: It was when I went off to college, to Stillwater, when I really got a chance to play music regularly. But I'll tell you this: My dad sent me to college to *keep* me from playing music. Let me explain. There was a place in Nashville called Opryland USA. It's a theme park, and every year they would go on a hunt, sifting through tens of thousands of auditioners, a bunch in each city, and they would pick a handful of people to come play there, kind of be in the regular cast of performers. My buddy wanted to be in it so bad. So I went with him to one of the auditions near us, and the lady running it said, "Both of you are applying, right?" I told her that it was just him. She said, "Well why don't you, don't you play?" So I just signed up. I saw pictures of the red, white, and blue suits for the Fourth of July, and it was like Walt Disney took over country music, just beautiful to my eyes. Then I get the letter, and, damn, I'm one of the chosen after this nationwide search. I go to my folks and I say, "Guys, I'm in, this is what I wanted!" Mom and Dad look at me and go, "No, you are going to be a sophomore in college. You are not going to Opryland, and you've got to get a summer job to pay for your college. You can't go there because it would cost us money if you go there. Like, they're not paying shit, and you can't go." I'm sitting there thinking, *You've just stabbed me in the back.* I can't believe they're not

2802 Opryland Drive
Nashville, Tennessee 37214
615-889-6600

February 18, 1981

Dear Garth

    This letter is to confirm your employment as a performer in the Entertainment Department of Opryland USA for the 1981 season at the rate of $5.361 per hour (new employee) or $5.913 per hour (former employee). Your rehearsals will begin on May 26, 1981 at 10:00 a.m. You will need to report to the employee's entrance of Opryland USA at 9:45 a.m. (see attached fact sheet).

    Please return this signed letter which will serve as a contractual commitment between yourself and Opryland USA. I have enclosed a self-addressed envelope for your convenience. Also enclosed is a copy of this letter for your files. Formal contracts will be signed during your orientation on May 26, 1981.

Sincerely,

John Haywood
Manager of Entertainment

Yes, I confirm my employment with Opryland USA
beginning Tuesday, May 26, 1981.

_____
Signature

Enclosure
JMH:slb

Opryland · The Grand Ole Opry

Entertainment properties of The National Life and Accident Insurance Company

going to let me go do this thing. Wasn't it clear to them that when I got to Opryland, they were going to give me billions of dollars and a record deal? But my parents made the right decision. As much as I hated to admit it.

TY ENGLAND: The first time I heard of Garth, in fact the first time I ever heard the name "Garth," would have been 1983, I believe. I had grown up with music, had musical ambitions myself, and by that time had moved to Oklahoma State University and pledged a fraternity with some musical buddies of mine from high school. I got in the fraternity, but it was a very uncomfortable situation for me. I was claustrophobic, and they had us all piled in one big room together. It didn't suit me well. So I de-pledged and kind of rambled around campus without a place to really live. I lost all my musical buddies in that deal. Around that same time I heard about an open mic night at the student union. So I got on the bill and was absolutely terrified once it was actually happening. I was playing

I WAS INTERESTED IN ANYONE WHO WANTED TO PLAY A LITTLE MUSIC.
It wasn't an exclusive club, no auditions, no membership fees. - g

a song, and the young lady running the open mic could tell I was just dreadfully nervous, so she walked up with a glass of water. I'm trembling from my inner core, and I proceed to pour the water all over me and my guitar. The crowd laughed, and it kind of broke the ice. I calmed down and sang a couple more songs. "Radio" by Don Williams and, I think, John Conlee's "Rose Colored Glasses." There were maybe a dozen people there, but after my performance a guy named Ted Larkin came up to me and goes, "Dude, you got to meet a friend of mine." He wrote down Garth's name and room number and phone number, handed it to me.

G: I was interested in anyone who wanted to play a little music. It wasn't an exclusive club, no auditions, no membership fees. *(laughs)* So I got to meet a lot of folks just because we were connected by the music. Like Ty England. Like Brian Petree. Randy Taylor. A long list of folks.

TY ENGLAND: I hear the phone pick up and instantly hear music in the background. Just as you'd hear Garth say it today, he goes, "Hello?" Always upbeat, uptempo. I told him, "Hey, you know I feel a little weird here, but a friend of yours told me I should give you a call." So he says, "Absolutely, come on over. Where are you at?" And it turned out that I was living exactly two floors above Garth's room. He was in 202, I was in 402. So I rode down the elevator and met Garth that day for the first time. I walked in the room, and there was a guy named Jim Blair that played mandolin, a good friend of ours that we lost named Bill Pierce was playing banjo, and there was Garth. They were all settled around this little tape recorder, a little Radio Shack thing on the floor between them. That was their studio. Garth invited me in, asked me, "What kind of music do you like?" I told him I was a big Don Williams fan. He goes, "Well play me something." I start playing "Listen to the Radio," and the guys kind of just fall in around me. Garth sings harmony, knows the song. My hair is standing on end just telling this story. It was thrilling for me to find somebody that loved music like I did. I asked if I could take that tape home, and Garth gave it to me. I gave that tape to my mother to hear. She asked me a couple times, "Who is this you're playing with?" I'd tell her his name is Garth, but she just didn't quite comprehend. She thought it was with an "F," so in her hand she wrote on that tape, "Ty and Garf." I may still have that tape.

It was thrilling for me to find somebody that
LOVED MUSIC LIKE I DID.
- TY ENGLAND

G: Ty ends up being my roommate . . . until the music got the better of the student within him. *(laughs)*

TY ENGLAND: Garth pulled some strings, and we ended up being roommates for a while. But I wasn't very studious once I got around Garth, I have to admit. My grades tanked. We'd taken a blanket and plastered it over our window so we could keep the sun out and just keep playing, like it was still night. Then I'd sleep through class. After a couple of semesters of that my dad said, "Son, I know you're having a lot of fun at OSU with your buddies, but I'm not paying for these grades anymore." I had to say goodbye to Garth, went home to Oklahoma City. But we made a promise to one another that if we ever had the chance to play music, really play it professionally, we'd bring the other guy along.

BRIAN PETREE: I was at Oklahoma State, living in Stout Hall. The farthest thing from my mind was that I'd ever work as a road manager for one of the biggest acts in history. But it had to start somewhere, right? Well, across the street there was another dormitory and a field. I'm not sure what the occasion was, but the university had put a trailer with some hay bales around it out in the middle of this field. There was going to be a talent show, so a couple of us in Stout Hall had gotten together and worked up a Jimmy Buffett song and some cowboy song, and we were going to join the talent show. We figured we'd probably win that thing, right? We go across to see whatever is going on, and there's Garth up there singing. He's up there by himself, him and his guitar, still with the beard and the feed cap, singing what he called "worthless originals." One of the kids with me points at Garth and goes, "Oh, he signed up for the talent show, too." My group went back and crossed our names off the list for that event. There's no way we are going up against this guy.

Playing there with just a guitar and a handful of people, some sober, some not, and you're all within 20 feet of each other, **THAT WAS SCHOOL.** -g

G: Brian Petree was in college at the same time as me. I was coming toward the end of my college years, when, I think, a guy named Randy Taylor, who wrote "Much Too Young," introduced me to him. Petree was a cowboy. He was a roper, and pretty serious about it. America and Japan had international alliances, and every year we would send a few ropers over to Japan to teach their children how to rope. Brian Petree was one of the ropers that they would send over. He's got this really sweet picture of himself in college, has this big thick handlebar mustache, like the guy on *Tombstone,* and he's squatting down and has this loop in the air. He's got this little Japanese kid in shorts and sandals beside him and Mount Fuji is in the background. But Petree wanted to write songs, so he just kind of drifted toward us. Turned out he was a bartender.

BRIAN PETREE: It was probably six months after that talent show that I went into Willie's Saloon and recognized that the same guy was in the back of this place singing.

G: Now, when graduation came, it turned out I was one class short of my degree. I got my picture taken with my tassel, but it wasn't official. Still don't know how it happened. But I had to go back up that summer after I graduated, just for that one course. That meant I had to live up there in Stillwater. I couldn't afford to drive back and forth. So I had two females who were roommates, who agreed to do a *Three's Company* thing with me, where I helped them with the rent and they would let me stay with them. That was when I went down to Willie's Saloon with my guitar, met a lady named Dolly, who was the owner's, Bill's, wife. She said, "Look, I want you to just come in on Wednesday, and let's just see what happens." I said okay. No money was discussed. I played one night, and she comes up to me and she goes, "You know, I really enjoyed myself." She says, "I'll hire you, how much you thinking?" I asked for a hundred bucks a night, which she thought was a little high, but she said she'd try. I played Willie's for three years. People will sometimes ask me, you know, "Where did it all start?" For me, I'll forever say it was Willie's Saloon, Stillwater, OK.

BRIAN PETREE: There were probably a dozen people at Willie's watching Garth up on the stage in his checked flannel shirt, playing his Ovation guitar and just doing what was contemporary in the day, Billy Joel and Don McLean and Gordon Lightfoot. Whatever anybody called out from the audience, he would play it, and that was just amazing. I sat there through the set, loving it, and talked to him afterwards. Told him how much I liked it. I wound up going back to Willie's a couple other times, just to watch him play. Turned out we had a mutual friend, Randy Taylor.

G: When you play for tips, you better know everything. The more you know, the more chances you have of the tip jar filling up. Even the stuff you may not like, you got to find a way to make it yours and sell it. So Willie's Saloon was a big thing for me, a time I learned a whole lot. Playing there with just a guitar and a handful of people, some sober, some not, and you're all within 20 feet of each other, that was school. If somebody starts to heckle, somebody starts to mouth off, everyone is watching how you're going to handle it. You learned fast, and if you didn't, you wouldn't last.

TRISHA YEARWOOD: I have a lot of respect and I'm almost jealous that he had that experience. We still talk about it a lot because when I got my record deal, I hadn't played in the clubs. Not like that. I learned in the studio. I didn't have the experience of singing in front of every kind of crowd you can imagine. I believe it's where Garth learned a lot about being a performer. You really get to know a lot about the art of performing by singing live in a small club. You find out what people like, what they don't like, what's going to work with a crowd, what's not going to work. Strange as it sounds, what works in a club of 100 people is going to work in an arena of 15,000. Even when Garth's making an album, he thinks of the live show and how those songs are going to flow and what they're going to do in a live setting, probably more than a lot of artists. I think it's one of the reasons why he is so successful. He learned a lot from playing in front of those club crowds, probably got the best training he could have had.

Tuesday it's
Free BEER
for Everyone
7-9

Thumpers

Then Enjoy LIVE ENTERTAINMENT
by Garth Brooks

Hear a variety of your favorite nostalgic
tunes and dance to Top 40 at Thumpers.
Come in tonight!

Ladies:
You never pay a cover at Thumpers

Proper Dress & ID Required   2021 N. Boomer

G: I can see the set list in my head. It was three legal-size pieces of paper, probably somewhere around 150-200 songs, everything from Slim Whitman to Elton John to David Allan Coe to Nitty Gritty Dirt Band, Jerry Jeff Walker to Peter, Paul and Mary and Billy Joel. You were up at that pulpit, that focal point, and you had to read the room, figure out what those people needed. That was your job.

BRIAN PETREE: Garth knew how to connect with the people, knew that being a performer was *about* the connection with the people. He wasn't entertaining himself, although he'll tell you he's the one having the best time up there . . . and it seems to be true! To this day, I'd say.

G: But before I was playing Willie's, I worked as a bouncer at The Tumbleweed. And even that was a part of my general education as an entertainer, you know? *(laughs)* As a bouncer, you've got 2,000 people on a crowded night, and you've got maybe 12 bouncers, at the most. You do that math. It could all go wrong. What you depend on is that 99.9 percent of people go there just to have a good time. They don't want any trouble. They want to unwind. Then, of course, you have your one or two that do their thing. You learn. You watch the people. You get to understand crowds better, people better. But for the most part, I pretty much ended up dancing most of the time. Girls would come up asking, and you'd just go dancing. It was awesome. You got to see, from the dance floor, what *packed* the dance floors. You got to see what kind of music did it. When the floor was empty, you took note of what song was playing. You were going to school without knowing it, I guess. But they would also have some big acts come there, including King George, George Strait. Everyone knew I loved him to death. So when he came to The Tumbleweed and the bouncers were assigned their spots, they gave me the southeast parking lot. Out there, you were lucky if you could hear the music. I guess they just knew I'd be all over him like a teenage girl. But they did get me a shirt, a You Look So Good in Love tour shirt. I wore that thing until it fell off me.

BOB DOYLE: All the pieces in Garth's history kind of add up, like every experience had a lesson somewhere in it. But, really, you could say that that holds true for all of us. The difference is that some people are looking for those lessons, looking to learn. And Garth always has been like that. He wasn't just sitting back and watching.

G: For me, there's no difference between playing for five people or five hundred thousand. None at all. It's still about getting it down to that one-on-one communication. It's maybe even a little *more* nerve-wracking to play for five people than it is for five hundred thousand. So those things you do as a college kid, you're doing as an adult. It's still all about entertaining. It's still about making people laugh and the second they start to laugh, that's when you hit them with the stuff that makes them cry.

> Garth knew how to connect with the people, knew that **BEING A PERFORMER WAS ABOUT THE CONNECTION WITH THE PEOPLE.** He wasn't entertaining himself, although he'll tell you he's the one having the best time up there. - BRIAN PETREE

I started to understand entertaining from all different kinds of levels. You can see great players. You can see great singer-songwriters. You can see great singers. And sometimes you can even get that all in one pot . . . and you *still* fall asleep watching them. But then there's that great *entertainer*. So the epiphany I had, or call it the theory that I'm working on right now is this: A good entertainer does what he or she wants to do onstage, so they might go off on this twelve-minute guitar solo and the crowd is kind of lost, but that entertainer is doing what they want to do onstage, which is a good thing. Or, alternatively, a good entertainer is someone who does what the crowd came to see, whether that entertainer wants to do it or not. But a *great* entertainer is lucky enough that what the crowd wants to see is the exact same thing that he or she wants to do. That's a great entertainer. And I got to tell you, it's not my place to say, but I do know I feel so comfortable onstage doing just what I believe the people came to see.

"A great entertainer is lucky enough that **WHAT THE CROWD WANTS TO SEE IS THE EXACT SAME THING THAT HE OR SHE WANTS TO DO. THAT'S A GREAT ENTERTAINER.**"

- g

In 1980, there were two very different movies about country music being screened in America's movie houses. Both did extremely well at the box office, a testament to the nation's lasting interest in sounds from America's heartland. But the one movie, *Coal Miner's Daughter,* couldn't have been more different from the other, *Urban Cowboy.* While *Coal Miner's Daughter* showed the gritty world from which country legend Loretta Lynn had come, revealing country music's past, *Urban Cowboy* starred John Travolta and seemed to be a reflection of country's future, its move toward a more pop sound. 1980 was also the year that Garth Brooks would graduate from Yukon High School and, come that next fall, leave Yukon for Oklahoma State in Stillwater. Country music would be on his mind. On the pop charts at the time, there was also plenty that appealed to the ncoming Oklahoma State freshman—Queen, Billy Joel, Fleetwood Mac, and Boston. And in the next year, a revolution was coming: MTV. For those who loved the visual side of popular music, and Brooks did, MTV would change the game—and not just in dance music and rock and roll but every genre, country music included. The surprise in it all was that the traditional sounds associated with Loretta Lynn and others of her generation weren't going to be washed away in the rush toward popular music's future. Quite the opposite. As the 1980s got underway, artists like Randy Travis, Ricky Skaggs, Dwight Yoakam, and Keith Whitley would join legends like George Strait and Reba McEntire to make it seem like traditional country might just be the "next big thing." They opened the doors wide enough for the next wave of traditionalists to come through . . . and, if those doors weren't opened wide enough already, they were about to be kicked off their hinges.

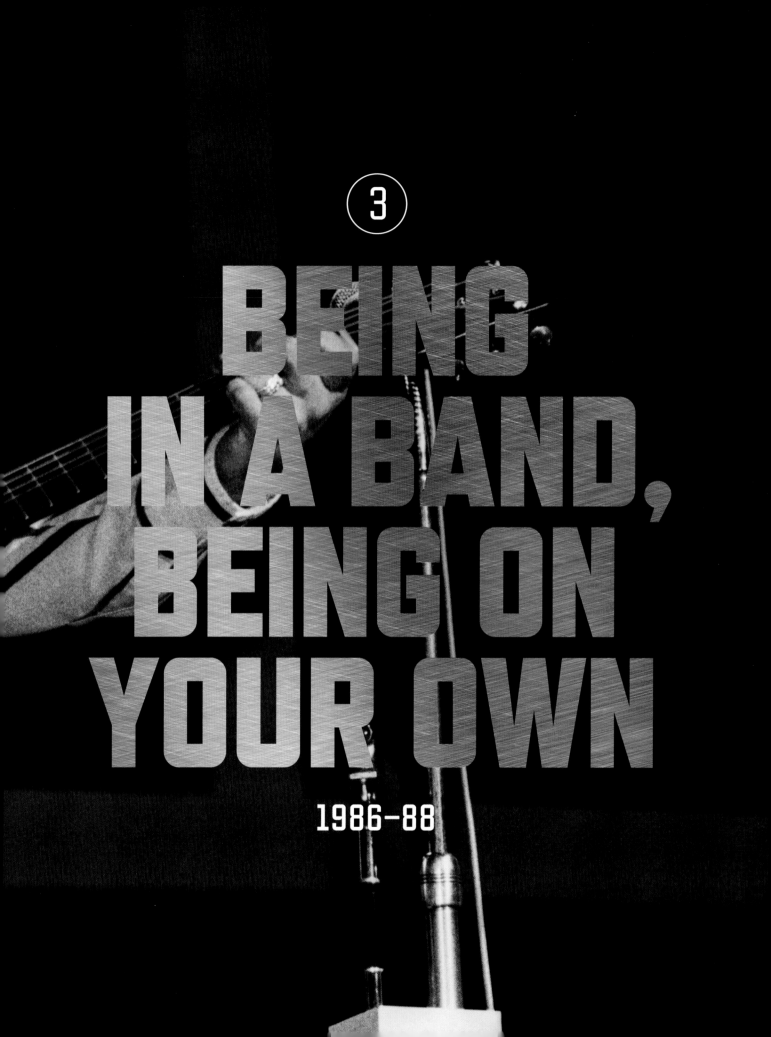

3

BEING IN A BAND, BEING ON YOUR OWN

1986–88

In 1985, Michael Jackson sent his album *Thriller* all the way to the top of the pop charts. It was a global phenomenon. They were moonwalking in Cairo. It didn't matter what genre a recording artist worked in, they all marveled at what he had done. But no one in country thought such a thing could happen to them. That's just not how it was. Country music didn't cross over like that. You pop the champagne corks for gold records, but you don't go to bed dreaming of platinum.

A year later, Garth Brooks appeared on television for the first time as the lead singer in a band called Santa Fe. It was the *A.M. Oklahoma* morning show. In a matter of years, that same Garth Brooks was going to surpass Michael Jackson in album sales. Traditional country under threat? That's not where the story was headed.

73

TO LEARN HOW TO LEAD A BAND, I FIRST HAD TO BE IN ONE,

just as a member of a band, for that on-the-job training. We were called Santa Fe. In the end, the band broke up, but it was a school I had to attend before the rest of this could happen. - g

BRIAN PETREE: I helped him get the Thumper's gig. Just like he helped me get a few bartending jobs. It was the first time his name was on a marquee, I think.

G: Thumper's was like Willie's, playing covers, me and a guitar. Where I could, I'd sneak in a few of what I called "worthless originals." That was the title for them. You know, "Time for another worthless original, folks." You'd do two or three a night because people would come there and you'd start to see the repeat business. That clientele now had faith in you, and they wanted you to take them somewhere that no other artist's music that they heard took them. They wanted to hear your voice, your point of view. So it was a very safe place to do some really . . . I don't want to call it immature, just really young stuff from a time when you hadn't matured yet as a writer. Your first shots at songwriting. There's not a songwriter that I know that doesn't roll their eyes at some of their first stuff. And one of the greatest things that we *didn't* have was cell phones. You could make your mistakes on a live audience. You could try the song out and see them drift away and go, "Well, that song's just not working." And no one had filmed it!

BRIAN PETREE: One time when we were still in college I got a phone call from Garth. He said, "Man, you need to go with us. We're driving out to . . ." He'll remember the city, I don't. But it was some two hours from Stillwater. He said we were driving out there because he found out Willie Nelson was going to be at this train station or a bus station.

I swear that was the story. We were going to go there, and Garth was somehow going to pitch him this song he'd written called "The Man Behind the Plow." I still remember the name of the song. *(laughs)* Garth said he just wanted somebody else to go along so we could all take turns driving. For some reason the trip never happened. But, I mean, this was eleven o'clock at night. Even then it was like, "If I could just get this song to Willie Nelson, it will go somewhere." He believed. So did I.

G: When touring acts came into town, you'd kind of get a sense of the bigger world. There was something out there . . . and here was a little evidence.

BRIAN PETREE: The Lazy E was in Guthrie. I was working as a bartender there. It was a big roping arena, that's essentially what it was, a rodeo arena with a bar on one end. I remember I was working and there was a roping event coming up. Actually, I was serving Wilford Brimley, because he's a roper. You know the actor Wilford Brimley? Anyway, I talked to whoever was managing and said, "Man, are you looking for entertainment?" They said that as a matter of fact they were, that they had Jerry Jeff Walker coming in and were looking for an opener. So I called Garth. By that time I knew of his ambitions, that he wanted to go to Nashville to be a singer-songwriter.

G: I love Jerry Jeff Walker. Sharing a stage with him? C'mon, of course I was in!

BRIAN PETREE: I was working that night. I remember Jerry Jeff sat in that same bar and changed his guitar strings, right up at the bar. I don't think Garth was there yet, but he played the show, just him and his guitar, like he was at Willie's. There was a twenty-by-twenty stage they'd drag out at the end of the arena. It was just a PA in a barn, really, so I'm sure the sound was awful. But Garth did a set. The big time. *(laughs)*

G: Well, it was the big time! I don't care what the gig is, if it's bigger than anything you've ever done . . . it sure as hell *is* the big time. But that's probably around the time I starting thinking more about what it would be like if I wasn't alone up there on that stage. It's all about connecting with your audience, whether that's three people or three hundred, but I started thinking, *What if those songs could get even bigger?*

BOB DOYLE: Garth has always used his eyes in an amazing sort of way. He'll look at you out there and connect, and it's a very natural thing for him. Whether he's up there by himself or with a band he can bring a room together. It's part of what he does, in a very comfortable way, to include you and to make this whole experience inclusive. I think he's always had this, as far back as Oklahoma. It's who he is as a person. It's not about you, the audience, pleasing him because he's onstage. It's about him giving that audience something of value. It's the old thing we've always said, "You can give them back their money but you can't give them back their time."

G: Dale Pierce was a shot put/discus thrower from Woodward, Oklahoma. This guy had a God-given talent as an athlete, so much so that he never worked out. *(laughs)* All we did was play music. And this guy could play banjo like nobody else, could just pick up anything. We started getting together with another cat named Jim Kelly. Jim was a hurdler that my brother Kelly introduced me to. It was Dale Pierce who came to me and said, "There's a group in town called the Skinner Brothers. You probably need to get with these guys and see if you can't take this to another level."

TY ENGLAND: In some ways, I don't think anyone was surprised when Garth kept moving it along. He loved the music, and he had a way of seeing where to go with it next.

G: It was three brothers, Craig, Tom and Mike Skinner. The Skinners were all about what I call muscle music. When Tom Skinner sat down at the table with me, it was so sweet, because the way he broke the ice, he said, "Let's put a band together." He didn't ask if I wanted to, didn't interview me like I was lucky to be with him. He just said, "Let's put a band together." That did everything.

They did Lynyrd Skynyrd kind of stuff, a lot of Southern rock. And then I'm a George Strait guy. So you put these two things together, these two sounds together, and now you've got George Strait singing, "I know a little 'bout love, and baby I can guess the rest." Things like "Cadillac, long, dark, shiny and black." But one of the Skinners played not just mean guitar but also fiddle. He played a kind of back porch fiddle, not

> # You can give them back their money but YOU CAN'T GIVE THEM BACK THEIR TIME. — BOB DOYLE

trained fiddle, like you knew he was a guitar player when he played that thing. So the Southern rock feel of the fuzzed-out guitar mixed with this fiddle and . . . all of a sudden there was this muscle in country music. Now you hear these guys play "Unwound" or "The Fireman" by George Strait. Or some Nitty Gritty Dirt Band, and it was something different. We went in these dance halls, and it was exactly what the places needed because during the breaks from the live band, the DJs would be playing rock and pop. We brought the rock and roll feel right into the live set, into the dance halls of Oklahoma. And you saw it, you saw it immediately. The dance floors were packed. The owners would go, "Boys, you set a record tonight on beer sales."

DAVE GANT: I met Garth several years before he hired me to play keyboards and fiddle in his band. It was in Oklahoma, a place called Bink's. He was in the opening act.

G: We picked up Jed Lindsay, a guitar player, there at Stillwater and a drummer named Troy Jones. Great guys. We called the band Santa Fe, and we played the Bamboo Ballroom in Enid, Oklahoma. We played Norm's in Ponca City. Graham's Central Station, Tulsa City Limits, The Tumbleweed. These are dance halls, anywhere from 1,200 to 2,000 capacity. They're like indoor basketball courts, where the dance floor's probably 100 feet by 200 feet. They're good-sized dance halls, and when they're packed—there is no fire code—so at the end of a college football game, say, or something like that, Mother's Day, whatever, there could be 2,000 people in a place that seats 1,200.

DAVE GANT: I was playing with Pake McEntire, Reba McEntire's older brother. We're playing a gig in Stillwater, with Garth in the opening act and Brian Petree as the bartender. We did sound check, then left to go eat, change clothes, all that. We come back, and the place was packed. Pake is like, "Yeah, we got 'em!" And there's Garth, playing with his band Santa Fe. He was great. The place was full, and he was singing George Strait, sounding like George Strait. He'd play James Taylor and sound like James Taylor.

Nobody knows what it takes to make it in this town. YOU LEARN IT WHEN YOU GET HERE. -g

G: I remember that show! Santa Fe was doing pretty good, starting to get a sound.

DAVE GANT: Garth stayed and listened to the Pake McEntire band. I guess that's how he knew that I did fiddle and keyboards.

G: There were some great local acts that played the dance halls in Oklahoma. There was a group called the Country Cousins that would soon turn into a group called Stone Horse. They were the real thing. Everybody loved them. They toured Arkansas and Texas, and they were a matching bow twin fiddle group, had the twin fiddle art down. And then there was a group called Steel Away that did a lot of covers, which everyone liked.

BRIAN PETREE: Around Stillwater there were a lot of these big dance places where you could see bands.

G: So you're a musician and it's like you're taking notes. You see that everyone wants to come see the Country Cousins because they're the real deal and they swing. Everyone comes to see Steel Away because they play all covers, big covers like, "If You're Gonna Play in Texas (You Gotta Have a Fiddle in the Band)." And the dance floor is packed, and you're just watching this. Then there was a guy named Jay Arnold, had the Jay Arnold Band. He was the one that you would have picked out of all of them like, *Oh, that's the business guy.* This guy is smart. He's savvy. He was a beautiful cat. He had a good voice. But you could just tell he was really good at his job. So you got to see all these different aspects of how this band thing works. You're thinking, well, if you put all of the best parts of these acts into one, you might get a machine that just *rolls.*

DAVE GANT: Just hanging out after the show, you could see that Garth was just what he is today—and has been as long as I've known him—real nice, real open. But I also sensed that he was taking it all in, wasn't missing the details.

G: You can watch and you can study. I remember Santa Fe fronted Dwight Yoakam in Stillwater. I watched Dwight Yoakam with a three-piece band and these guys . . . they were having more fun than the people in the bar were having! And I'm going, *hmmm,* because I'm a George Strait guy, and Strait just sings. I was a bluegrass guy, too, and bluegrass guys don't laugh. They don't even smile, not at that point. But I'm watching this guy have a great time, and I'm going to myself, *Well, shit, this guy is playing damn straight country music, real Bakersfield sound, and these guys are having a blast. Why can't we do that?* The guitar player, Pete Anderson, was tearing it up, and they all had the old kind of string ties on. The drummer was fucking phenomenal but had just a snare, maybe one tom, one crash, and that's all. They had a bass player that looked like he was seven foot tall, just kicking it. These guys were lean, made a lot of noise and had a lot of fun. Yoakam really yanked my chain when it came to, *Hey, that's what I want to do!*

STEVE COX: I didn't know Garth back then, this was before we toured together with Trisha in the '90s, but I get the feeling he hasn't changed a lot. So when it comes to the people showing up to see us play, they're coming to see that man. And what he wants, what he wants to do . . . *should you do it?* Well, it seems he's been right about everything so far. So my feeling is that what he wants to do up there on the stage is what you need to do. You better get out of your own fucking head for a second and listen to the master.

G: There were two trips to Nashville, the first lasting only twenty-four hours, with me running fast as hell back to Oklahoma. But I went back again, this time with the band, with Santa Fe. And I'll tell you, all five of us came to this town scared out of our fricking wits, no money and all with a different opinion of what it would take to make it in this town. And the crazy thing was, all five of us were wrong. Nobody knows what it takes to make it in this town. You learn it when you get here.

BOB DOYLE: I think one of the reasons it's so important for any musician to go to a place like L.A. or New York or Nashville, where music is made at such a high professional level, is that you truly get a perspective on what you're going to have to do to be part of the game.

G: It's five guys who are scared, two of us are married, there's a child, and there's a cat and a dog. All in the same house. It's a band house. Scared to death. We all got jobs, working during the day and then, at night, we're going to The Sutler, we're going to Douglas Corner, and we're trying to play gigs. We played a gig downtown, I can't remember the name of the place. Pat Alger, who would later be a writer on "Unanswered Prayers," "The Thunder Rolls," and some others, mentioned going to this gig. He said the place was kind of seedy. That was putting it gently. It was a rough ass gig, downtown. And it just got frustrating, man, real quick. We played covers. We played originals. But we could never agree on when to play the covers and when to play the originals, and then there's a thing in town that says, "Play in Nashville, stay in Nashville." That saying scared everybody.

BOB DOYLE: You know, in almost any band there has to be a leader, there has to be a point of view that dominates the sound. Otherwise, it drifts and the egos conflict and, finally, the sounds conflict, you lose the point of view. It's hard. Of course, Garth still has a band. His band has been there forever, right up there with him and a very important part of the experience. They know each other well, as people and musicians, but they are playing Garth's music. It's his point of view that gives the live show its focus.

BRUCE BOUTON: I played pedal steel on the records and didn't join the road band until later. But I have to say, I've worked with a lot of bands over the years, and I've been in more than I'd want to count, and Garth, as a leader, leaves as much room for his band members as anybody I've seen. And that's the trick: to give the players space to be themselves without failing to be a leader. If you can pull *that* off, it might just work. Assuming you have the songs and the talent. 'Cause you gotta have a leader, whether you're the Rolling Stones, Bruce Springsteen and the E Street Band, U2. If they're still together . . . well, that probably means there's someone in that role doing a good job of it.

G: In Santa Fe, you had Tom Skinner and you had Garth Brooks. Tom Skinner was always the leader of The Skinner Brothers. But this was Santa Fe. We were a democracy, five different angles on this thing we were trying to do, so that's why we didn't get far . . . we just all had our different ideas. And, then, we were getting shopped for a record deal and it wasn't the band, it was one of the guys in the band. And one of the other guys said, "Man, they're not going to let us stay with him if he signs a record deal. They are going to hire hotshot crack musicians." And again we were all wrong on what would have happened. They hired the hotshot crack musicians to make the records, but the band is whoever your buddies are that you kind of do your thing with. Before we could find that out, though, they all just dispersed. Some of them went back home, some of them stayed here, just worked their jobs. But it all fell apart, and that was hard.

TRISHA YEARWOOD: I think that the guys in Santa Fe really encouraged him. I wasn't there, but my take on it is that Garth was developing a lot of skills fronting that band, how to talk to a crowd, how to lead. I think it shaped him, but also helped him to become his own person. I'm sure he was learning that he really was a leader. Sometimes someone in a group just naturally emerges and is ready to go to the next level. That person doesn't get to know how that's going to go, but I'm sure they all saw that if anybody was going to do it, it was Garth. But I also know that Garth is such a loyal person that, as much as going solo was what he needed to do, it probably wasn't easy to do. But if you have that fire, that desire, that drive to do it, even if you're scared, it just doesn't leave you, and you finally have to figure out a way to do it.

YOU BETTER GET OUT OF YOUR OWN FUCKING HEAD
for a second and listen to the master. - STEVE COX

G: Looking back now, you know, it was one of the greatest gifts I ever had, getting to be part of a band and getting to learn. There are things I learned then that I'm still using today. Everyone has an opinion, and you try to represent everybody, but, at the same time, somebody needs to sit at the steering wheel. But with Santa Fe, we had a dream we shared for a while there. Does some part of your heart break with each step forward? Yes. Then, over time, something new grows in its place.

BOB DOYLE: I don't know whether they gave up or the dream they came to town with just couldn't be realized. Your sense of who you are and what you're doing has to step up a grade or two, and quickly. There's a lot of musicians here and, wow, there's a lot of good songwriters, so you've got to be great. That's a new kind of pressure to people moving here. When I met him, Garth was writing. I met Garth through a friend, Stephanie Brown. It was through the introduction of a tape from Stephanie. He was a man with some good songs, playing a guitar.

TY ENGLAND: Garth and Bob had a really good working relationship. Garth was willing to bleed for the cause, and Bob was there to tell him where to give blood.

TRISHA YEARWOOD: I think when he met Bob, Bob saw something in Garth that maybe Garth didn't even see in himself yet. We all need somebody to encourage us and

> Garth and Bob had a really good working relationship. Garth was willing to bleed for the cause, and **BOB WAS THERE TO TELL HIM WHERE TO GIVE BLOOD.**
> - TY ENGLAND

kind of tell us our instincts about what we want to do are right. Bob did that for him. It was kind of Garth and Bob against the world, especially in the beginning before he got his record deal. They stood together as every label in Nashville passed on Garth, until he sang at The Bluebird.

G: Now I'm with Bob. He hears my demo, thinks there's something there. So I'm making a draw as a writer. I'm working at a boot place, and I'm cleaning a church. Sandy is working at the boot place with me, and that's how we're kind of making ends meet at this point. Stephanie Brown is my landlord, and I'm singing demos for a guy named Kent Blazy, just singing demos for people around town, trying to make ends meet. And as far as playing shows is concerned, I'm back to where I was: me up there with a guitar. And I've always been comfortable with that.

BOB DOYLE: The first time I heard him perform was in my office, sitting across my desk from me, playing a couple songs. After that, it was a matter of him getting on songwriter nights at places like The Bluebird. In either situation, you could see that this person knew how to communicate a song. The Bluebird is really sort of a sterile writer's environment, where they shush everybody, and Garth could get the crowd on their feet,

which is not a typical response at The Bluebird. Early on I was beginning to see strong hints of what he was capable of in the bigger sense of it all. I've always maintained that the really great acts tend to come out of the clubs. They've cut their teeth engaging audiences that are just standing right there, just in front of the stage. And Garth had done all that early on. You could see it.

MARK GREENWOOD: The Bluebird was a very small club in a strip mall. I think it was a two-drink minimum. You would see a variety of singer-songwriters. But it was really for songwriters. I think they would load some names up, to get people in the door, and then use that attention to shine some light on a writer they thought was up-and-coming. You got songs and can sing? You show up and you try to get booked there. And get heard.

TRISHA YEARWOOD: If you're playing a songwriter night in the round with four or five other people, you're not only in a small group in a small setting, you're playing with just a guitar, no band behind you. You're naked in front of a crowd. But you're also a writer, singing songs that you've written, doubly vulnerable. You're not only saying, *I'm going to sing something*, now you're saying, *I'm also going to be saying something.* I don't do that. That's scary. Especially in this town, because Nashville is really built on songwriting.

G: At The Bluebird you were protected. Amy Kurland ran the place with love but a strict hand. Songwriters were worshipped, even more than artists. The important relationships you would make inside that house, inside that room, were with other songwriters. That was the place, the safe place for songs. There were the other rooms, like Douglas Corner and The Sutler. At The Sutler you were kind of at the mercy of everybody. You didn't know who you're going to see, what kind of clientele you were going to meet. And I loved that place, too. In between those two was Douglas Corner. At Douglas Corner, you were safe, but like The Sutler, you never knew who you were going to be playing for. Those three places are the reason I'm standing here today, because of the people I met and the relationships that came of it. Where there was live music . . . there was always something good. I've had times when everything went to shit, and the thing that saved me every time was live music, playing these songs in front of other people. In so many ways, the churches in my life are those places where people are playing music for other people. There's some kind of truth that lives there.

TY ENGLAND: Garth and I had this pact. I remember him saying to me one night in the dorm when we were roommates, he said, "You know, pal, if I ever really make it in this business, I want you to be there." And, kind of like a little brother might sound, I looked back at Garth and said, "Well, if I ever make it in this business I want you to be there, too." Of course, I was working at a Sherwin-Williams paint store back home, and he was in Nashville. So I'll leave it to you to guess who got there first. *(pause)* That's right, Garth signed a record deal. And damn if he didn't call me the day he signed with Capitol Records and say, "Pal, if you're really thinking you want to do this, you got to pack your things and get out here with me." I mean, on his big day he . . . he was thinking about someone else, and he put in that call. It still gives me chills.

BOB DOYLE: That's the way it goes with Garth.

TY ENGLAND: But still, I had a decision to make. I'm not from show business. I was working for a company that wanted to elevate my career and pay me considerably more money. I'm thinking about being a disappointment in my parents' eyes. They helped me find my way through college just to hear, "Oh, by the way, I'm going to chase this absurd musical dream in Nashville." For my own part, I'd always put entertainers on pedestals. And the people I was huge fans of did things different than I did, they were better than me, more talented, whatever. I didn't think, deep down in my soul, that I could ever

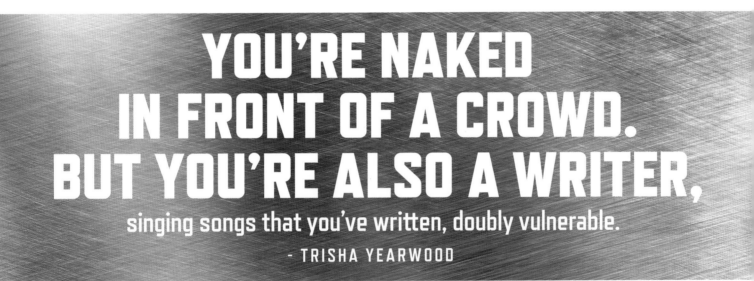

YOU'RE NAKED IN FRONT OF A CROWD. BUT YOU'RE ALSO A WRITER,
singing songs that you've written, doubly vulnerable.
- TRISHA YEARWOOD

really do what they do. Strange as it might sound, I had a real dilemma. I told Garth I had to think about it, asked him how quick I need to give an answer. He goes, "As quick as possible." I slept on it that night. Then, the next morning, I went into work and told my boss at Sherwin-Williams that I was giving my two weeks notice. Then I called Garth and told him what my plans were. I had this 1954 GMC truck that my dad and I had built. It was the only vehicle I had. So, one Saturday morning, I loaded all my things into the old jalopy, and started driving to Nashville.

"I'VE HAD TIMES WHERE EVERYTHING WENT TO SHIT, AND THE THING THAT SAVED ME EVERY TIME WAS LIVE MUSIC."

- g

BLUEBIRD SONGWRITER NIGHT AUDITIONS

DATE: _June 6, 1987_

NAME: _Garth Brooks_   PHONE: ~~(405)531-~~?
                                          865-
ADDRESS: _104 Forrest Meadows Ct._   9642
Hendersonville, TN.

NAME OF AUDITION SONG: _Calm before storm_

WHAT INSTRUMENT DO YOU PLAY? _guitar_

PLANNED INSTRUMENTATION FOR THE SHOW _____

_____

WHERE ARE YOU FROM? _Oklahoma_

HOW LONG HAVE YOU BEEN IN NASHVILLE? _1 month_

EXPERIENCE (include awards won, publishing companies worked
for, claims to fame, other music background):

won Opryland Talent Search in 1981

_____

_____

_____

OTHER INFORMATION I NEED THE BLUEBIRD TO KNOW: _____

_____

_____

QUESTIONS: _____

_____

These questions are to help us remember you, and to give us
good information for your introduction on stage. We would
like to keep this information up to date so please let us
know (in writing) about anything new we should add.

THANKS FOR PLAYING THE BLUEBIRD!!!!

*Amy —
You'll never know how much
you helped me. I owe you!
Just Hodd b...
Garth Brooks*

BOB DOYLE: At first Capitol Records turned us down. Just like so many other labels. Capitol changed their minds when Lynn Schults saw Garth perform live. It was at The Bluebird. Lynn saw what I saw. What the world was going to see.

G: I saw Bob Doyle in a TV interview once—I wasn't in the interview, was just watching—and he says something like, "This guy is not afraid of losing." And I went, holy shit, that's exactly right. I'm not . . . because no one's ever made me feel like losing made me a loser. It made me a trier, and they pulled harder for me.

IT WAS AT THE BLUEBIRD. LYNN SAW WHAT I SAW. WHAT THE WORLD WAS GOING TO SEE.

- BOB DOYLE

BOB DOYLE: Later Garth did a showcase for Capitol. He'd made the first record with Allen Reynolds. And all of a sudden we were stepping up. This was a showcase for thirty or forty people from the label. And I'm seeing Garth onstage with a band for the first time. All of my experience with him up to that point was really about the song and the creation of the song, the presentation of the song in its rawest form. I knew he'd come to town with a band, that he's played for a number of years back in Oklahoma, that this wasn't his first rodeo. But I hadn't experienced this part of it to the degree that I was about to. And a label showcase in a rented space is a very sterile environment, hard to get the energy level up. Then he knocked us out, like, *This isn't a young artist who just got signed.* It was so impressive to me. I thought, *Wow, if this is a starting point, who knows where this could go?*

ON THE ROAD... AT LAST!

4

1989–90

1989 was a big year for country music.

George Strait, The Judds, Randy Travis, all were going strong. But a new class of artists was on the rise. It included Alan Jackson, Travis Tritt, Clint Black, and Garth Brooks. From that point on, however, it was up to the artists to differentiate themselves. That took work, on the road, at radio stations, wherever the word could be spread. If you wanted a career, it meant setting everything but the music aside. If you weren't ready to give everything you had, there were no guarantees that you'd still be there a few years later.

When Garth Brooks and his band hit the road to support his debut release, they made a special connection in Texas. The Lone Star State had long been a place for Nashville's renegades to go and cut loose a little more than home might allow. Texas was ready for Garth Brooks. From the release of "Much Too Young (To Feel This Damn Old)," Texas was a kind of launchpad for Brooks. And in time, what happened there would happen . . . everywhere.

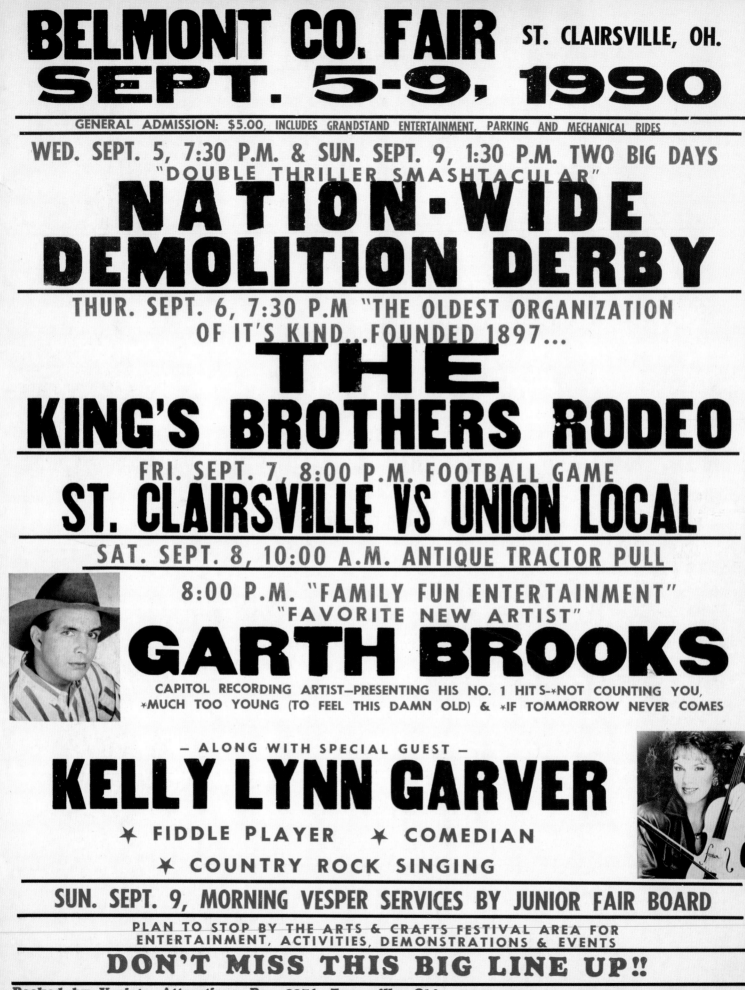

BELMONT CO. FAIR
ST. CLAIRSVILLE, OH.
SEPT. 5-9, 1990

GENERAL ADMISSION: $5.00, INCLUDES GRANDSTAND ENTERTAINMENT, PARKING AND MECHANICAL RIDES

WED. SEPT. 5, 7:30 P.M. & SUN. SEPT. 9, 1:30 P.M. TWO BIG DAYS
"DOUBLE THRILLER SMASHTACULAR"
NATION-WIDE DEMOLITION DERBY

THUR. SEPT. 6, 7:30 P.M "THE OLDEST ORGANIZATION
OF IT'S KIND...FOUNDED 1897...
THE KING'S BROTHERS RODEO

FRI. SEPT. 7, 8:00 P.M. FOOTBALL GAME
ST. CLAIRSVILLE VS UNION LOCAL

SAT. SEPT. 8, 10:00 A.M. ANTIQUE TRACTOR PULL

8:00 P.M. "FAMILY FUN ENTERTAINMENT"
"FAVORITE NEW ARTIST"
GARTH BROOKS
CAPITOL RECORDING ARTIST—PRESENTING HIS NO. 1 HITS-*NOT COUNTING YOU,
*MUCH TOO YOUNG (TO FEEL THIS DAMN OLD) & *IF TOMMORROW NEVER COMES

— ALONG WITH SPECIAL GUEST —
KELLY LYNN GARVER

★ FIDDLE PLAYER   ★ COMEDIAN
★ COUNTRY ROCK SINGING

SUN. SEPT. 9, MORNING VESPER SERVICES BY JUNIOR FAIR BOARD

PLAN TO STOP BY THE ARTS & CRAFTS FESTIVAL AREA FOR
ENTERTAINMENT, ACTIVITIES, DEMONSTRATIONS & EVENTS
DON'T MISS THIS BIG LINE UP!!

Booked by Variety Attractions—Box 2276, Zanesville, Ohio 43702-2276 614/453-0188 or 453-0394

WE WERE YOUNG

...and we were ready to stay out there forever.
-g

G: When it came to putting a band together, the first call goes out to Ty England, my college roommate. He comes to Nashville about six months before we get the full band together.

TY ENGLAND: One of the first things we got to do was the *Midnight Opry*. I think that's what it was called. It was just me and Garth. I still have a photo of us standing backstage at the Grand Ole Opry with my old guitar, the one I had at college. Neither one of us had any money to get new instruments. They put us onstage at like 3 a.m. It was just a radio show, wasn't televised. But I remember walking out, getting to center stage, and there was a circle they had cut out of the floor of the original Grand Ole Opry stage. They said all the greats stood in that circle. I remember thinking, *Man, that's where Hank Williams stood, that's where Hank stood.* My grandfather had taught me to love Hank Williams. And there I was, sharing the floorboards with him.

G: It's not like there's a point at which you feel like, *We've arrived!* It's just glimmers. Little moments, flashes. But we had this record coming out, something we were proud of, and we were just aching to play it live.

"It wasn't about having the best players so
GET ALONG TOGETHER ON A

much as wanting a group of guys who could

BUS FOR 300 DAYS A YEAR."

- MIKE PALMER

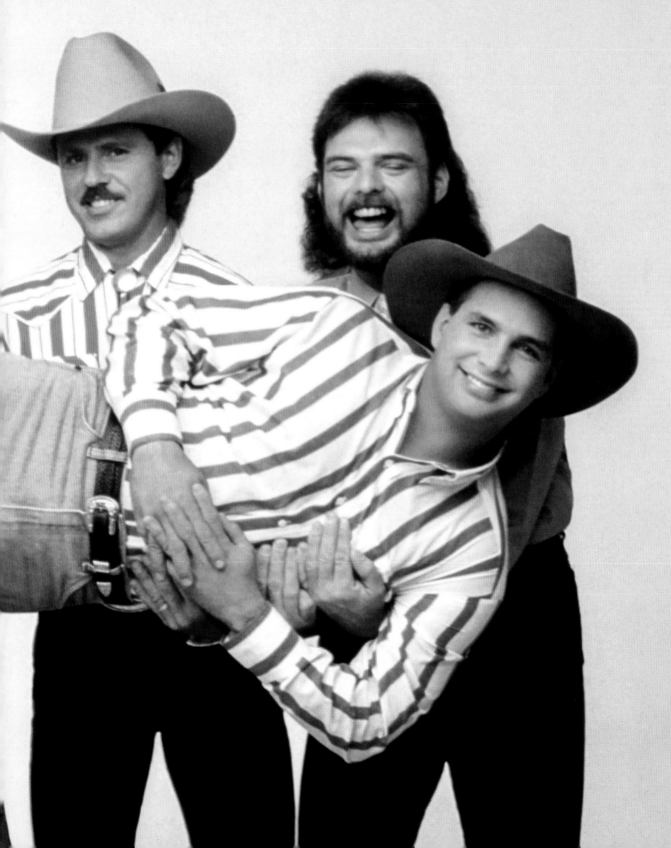

TY ENGLAND: I was dreadfully nervous there at the Opry. I had learned to harmonize pretty well with Garth. I probably didn't have the range I needed, but that came to me once we started doing it night after night. But sometimes I still wake up at night shaking, thinking about being on those stages, singing. That night I think we played "Much Too Young." That's the first time I remember Garth and I actually performing his music onstage.

G: I'm selling boots, and I run into a guy named James Garver. He's a guitar player. Actually, he was a fiddle player, that's why I brought him in. He introduced me to a guy named Steve McClure, a steel player. Both guys are from Kansas. So, me and Ty and James and Steve would sit down and play a little bit. We'd play in the basement of the apartment Sandy and I were renting from Stephanie Brown. Stephanie said she knows a bass player named Tim Bowers from North Carolina. So, there were the basic pieces, all coming together. Around that time I'm writing with Leigh Reynolds. I said to Leigh that I need a utility guy that plays keyboards, plays everything. He tells me about a guy from Oklahoma named David Gant who played keyboards and fiddle. I come to find out I'd opened for Dave in Oklahoma, when he played in Pake McEntire's band. So, I'd actually met this Dave Gant guy Leigh was telling me about.

DAVE GANT: So, Pake had us out on tour with Reba and Randy Travis, opening up on a pretty big deal of a tour. That's part of what got me closer to Nashville.

G: Dave Gant was playing with Pake McEntire on a Reba McEntire/Randy Travis tour when he met Leigh Reynolds. Leigh was Reba's bandleader at the time.

DAVE GANT: Thanks to Leigh, I got a call from Garth. We met up, and Garth gave me rough mixes of "The Dance," "Not Counting You," "Tomorrow Never Comes," and "Much Too Young." I thought, *this* is cool. Turned out he had some dates coming up with the studio band backing him, but his fiddle player, Robby Hajacos, was doing sessions 24/7 and his piano player, Bobby Wood, was out with The Highwaymen. I said, "Let's go, I'm in." I went out with Mike Chapman, Milton Sledge, and Chris Leuzinger and played with those guys. We did a festival in, I think, Johnson City, Tennessee, then the first big show was Detroit. After that, we'd start doing dates with the road band, which was, I think, almost complete by that time.

G: The only thing we got left to find is the drummer. And it's Steve McClure that says, "Hey, there's a kid from Florida, kind of working with this other artist right now. He's a really nice guy." His name is Mike Palmer.

MIKE PALMER: I moved to Nashville from outside of Tampa, in the middle of '88, to work with a guy named Clyde Foley Cummins. His grandfather was Red Foley. I met

Clyde in Florida at a fair and he told me, "Can you be up here in two weeks?" Not too long after that, Steve McClure came out to play guitar, and he was already playing steel and some guitar with Garth, working the songs up that they were recording. So, he mentions Garth to me. I said, "What? How do you spell that?" I'd never heard that name. Steve tells me he's on Capitol Records and he's looking for a drummer, asked if I minded him throwing my name in the hat. So, I was like, sure.

TY ENGLAND: I was young and dumb and could have cared less about learning. That early on I was just living in the moment, in all honesty. I was getting to play with a band and do things I just hadn't gotten to do, ever. Mike Palmer and I hit it off really good. I mean, we live in two different worlds now since I left Garth's band, but he was probably the one I was closest to on the road, especially in the absence of Garth, who got real busy real fast.

MIKE PALMER: Garth gave me a cassette to listen to the songs. There was one called "Nobody Gets Off in This Town" that I just loved, the creative writing, my kind of thing. And "If Tomorrow Never Comes" I thought was a big hit. And "The Dance" and a few other songs on there that I really liked. I figured if a couple of those would get out on the radio, he might have a career.

THAT EARLY ON I WAS JUST LIVING IN THE MOMENT
... I was getting to play with a band and do things I just hadn't gotten to do, ever. - TY ENGLAND

G: The first time we get together as a band, with all those people, is in Bob Doyle's office. But we just hang out. The second time we meet there we play as a unit. And, frankly, we're not sounding very good at all.

MIKE PALMER: I give Garth a lot of credit for a lot of stuff. Especially in hindsight, I understand some of the things he did. Our first meeting, between the band that he had already put together and myself, was at Bob Doyle's office. I set up everything, and then we didn't even play. We all just sat around and talked and just laughed and went out on the front porch. I don't remember playing until the second time we got together. So, I began to see it wasn't about having the best players so much as wanting a group of guys who could get along together on a bus for 300 days a year, because Garth wanted to work. He's always been, I think, wise beyond his years.

G: It's not happening, just not sounding right, then Dave Gant comes in with a piano/fiddle thing, which takes Garver over to guitar, and we kick off "Not Counting You." Bob Doyle comes flying through the door and he goes, "That's it! There's the club sound you're looking for." So, we were all pretty excited that, okay, at least now we have a structure. But do we have any gigs? The first show we booked was a thing called Spam Jam at an amphitheater here in town, I think it was called Starwood Amphitheatre. We were like the opening of twelve or fifteen other acts behind us.

I JUST LOVE GETTING IN A VAN WITH A BUNCH OF STINKY GUYS,
laugh your ass off, go to the club, eat shitty food that's been there for three days, the bologna has the rainbow on it. -g

TY ENGLAND: I was a real shy kind of kid. Even that night we played the Opry, I stood there with my guitar and probably looked at my boots all night. But when we played this thing called the Spam Jam, that is my awakening in the band. It was an outdoor amphitheater, midday, and no one is there. We went up and did, I think, a twenty-five minute performance, so probably five or six songs. I stood up there and I played my guitar part and I sang my part, but I wasn't selling it. Once I let go a little bit, then it got easier. But I think when we first hit the road there were still a lot of rough edges. But we did forge our pathway, through touring, just relentless touring.

G: There weren't many people there at Spam Jam, just a sprinkling. It was a little rainy, kind of drizzling. I really don't remember much of it. I can see as I'm thinking about it. I can see the backstage, all that stuff. But then you get to get in the van, a nine-passenger van with seven guys and all your gear. *(laughs)* I can see *that*. And, man, I'm telling you the word "fantastic" is not good enough for it. I mean it when I say this, *I'm a woman's guy.* I love women. Worship them. With that said, I love guys so fucking much. I just do. I love to work with them. I love to hang with them. I just love getting in a van with a bunch of stinky guys, laugh your ass off, go to the club, eat shitty food that's been there for three days, the bologna has the rainbow on it. And then these girls show up for the boys in the band to play for . . . and it's the greatest thing. And thus it begins. We start with a barn in Sanford, Florida. Well, we start with the KC Opry, with Tuffy Williams and the KC Opry, then Sanford, Florida, and on and on. We become a band.

DAVE GANT: At the first few shows there'd be more people working security than in the crowd.

BOB DOYLE: The character that needs to be introduced here is Joe Harris. Joe picked up the phone and asked Garth and I to come over and visit with him. He was a booking agent at Buddy Lee Attractions. We went over there, met him, Garth sang in his office . . . and Joe was sold. Joe had an unbelievable reputation amongst the buyers and was able to introduce us to a lot of business. Now it wasn't high-paying, $1,000, $1,500, $2,500 at the big gig. But it got us in front of a ton of people. One of the things Garth said to Joe was, you know, "Work us, we're ready to get out there."

G: So, now you're working for guys like George Moffett. George Moffett was probably the busiest promoter out there, one of the guys that chewed on the cigar, always. You'd pull into a place like Jamboree in the Hills and he brings out sandwiches, and you're like, "Man, we don't have to pay for these or nothing?" He goes, "No, have them all." And then, as he's leaving, under his breath he says, "They're what Travis Tritt's bunch didn't eat yesterday." *(laughs)* We're all looking at each other . . . then we just tear into them. Like, we're actually getting to eat food while playing music!

MIKE PALMER: Pretty soon, we're hitting a lot of the Texas ballrooms that held 1,000, 1,200, 1,500 people. They're huge, and you're traveling three or four hundred miles between sometimes. Garth's popularity was only just starting to pick up, so we didn't always have a full house. But something was happening. We played "Much Too Young (To Feel This Damn Old)" three times some nights because, *Oh, they recognized that one and danced to it, so let's play it again*! By the second round of the Texas ballrooms, everything was burning, so the crowds were getting good. Cutting our teeth in that kind of environment really helped us grow as a group.

G: We started out driving in a van. We had no crew and just took turns driving. I remember at one point it's Dave Gant's turn to drive. Now Gant is the old man in the band at thirty years old. He's not driving ten minutes when he starts to fall asleep. James Garver notices it first. The van crosses the line, comes back, crosses again, just . . . you have to tell him to pull over. We get someone else behind the wheel. It would be ten full years later that we would learn, *because* Dave was the "old man," he knew that's how he got out of driving if he didn't want to. *(laughs)* We all kind of learned from him. But we were getting ready to leave vans. At that early show at the Kansas City Opry, we got to see a bus for the first time ever. We were opening for a guy named J.C. Crowley, and we were just looking at his bus parked in the lot. It was empty except for the driver, and

we must have been salivating, because he asked if we would want to come on and see this thing. We got to go on, got to pull the door back and see the ice in the refrigerator. Everyone's like, "Oh, wow, here's the bunks!" Bunks, what are bunks?

DAVE GANT: The first bus was a special one. The driver's name was Wild Bill Coking. I remember we were going to Dallas, it may have been a Cowboys gig, but we were supposed to leave at noon. Of course, Bill shows up at 2 p.m. It was supposed to be what, ten or twelve hours? We got there in like eight or nine. He made up the two hours. Garth called him Fire Tires Coking. That bus was crazy. It stunk like vitamins, which Bill sold on the side. Stunk like piss and diesel fuel. But it was a deal, like a buck and a quarter a day or something.

G: It was disgusting and it was incredible. The driver sold herbs, that was kind of his deal. It smelled kind of garlicky. But then we found out there was some kind of diesel leak in the floors. So you'd walk out onstage and everybody's clothes smelled like the bus. Then we found out, pretty quickly, it didn't have reverse. If you overshot somewhere or had to get the bus out, everybody had to pile out and push. I'm telling you, it's the bus every band should start out in. But from there we went to Nitetrain, which was one of the biggest bus leasers here in Nashville. We just released our second single, and things were beginning to heat up.

> Pretty soon, we're hitting a lot of the Texas ballrooms that held
> # 1,000, 1,200, 1,500 PEOPLE.
> - MIKE PALMER

MIKE PALMER: We were starting to feel like winners because these people in the clubs are loving us back.

DAVE GANT: I remember we were in Texas, again, finished our sound check, ate, went and cleaned up, came back to the club . . . and we couldn't find space in the lot to park the bus anywhere. Garth was like, "Who's playing here?" *(laughs)* We go in there and, lo and behold, "Much Too Young" had become some kind of Texas anthem, and we didn't know it. Garth was huge in Texas. That club was packed out.

MIKE PALMER: Every night we would go out and sign autograph after autograph, for hours on end sometimes. We'd sign for anybody that wanted something signed, as many things as they wanted signed. We were spending probably the bulk of our day with our fans at that point, really getting to know them. And as things pick up, we also start to get some crew members on with us. The road family starts to grow.

DAN HEINS: It was a lot of fun back then. It was *real*. I run sound now, but for a minute there I was the only person on the crew, which meant I did whatever came my way.

HE KNOWS WHAT TO DO,
and you can tell that he loves it. - DAN HEINS

BRIAN PETREE: I was living in Austin, Texas, and I hear he's playing at a place called The Lumber Yard in Pflugerville, Texas. He's on the one bus, and I went by to see him, just to say hi. I think Dan Heins was the only crew guy. And Garth was like, "Dude, you're here, this is great! Are you ready to get on the bus now?" He told me they need a guitar tech. I'm like, "Yeah, absolutely." I jumped on the bus a day later, and that was almost thirty years ago. I think I told Garth, "Yeah, you know what, yeah, I'll do it for a year."

DAN HEINS: They were all headline bar gigs at that time. But they started to get more and more packed as that year went on. He'd just come out with another single, "If Tomorrow Never Comes," and that went to number one. He was on the radio quite a lot. I remember driving back to Wichita after they dropped me off at my car in Arkansas, and you couldn't go ten minutes without hearing a Garth, either "Much Too Young" or "If Tomorrow Never Comes." We'd get back on the bus after a show, and we'd all sit there. We weren't leaving without Garth. And where's Garth? He's outside in the parking lot signing autographs, with a line around the building. So, he would sign autographs until every one of those people was gone. We wouldn't leave the gig until four or five in the morning sometimes because he would not leave as long as somebody was standing out there wanting an autograph. But I think people meet him, and he's actually there in the moment with them. He's not looking past them or through them, trying to figure out how many more people he's got to do. He's sharing a moment and they feel it. This artist has never been handled by a manager telling him what to do. He knows what to do, and you can tell that he loves it.

BRIAN PETREE: Now when I saw him play that first time, he's killing it out there, swinging and running around, just got the crowd right with him. I was blown away. He had the whole crowd with him. He was running the show that night. To see that energy, and the way the band was enjoying it. It was a different Garth to me. Or the same Garth, but on a new stage. I thought maybe he'd act different. But, when he came off the stage . . . same Garth. So, yeah, I signed on. Then it was an adventure. And, in the beginning, one hell of a lot of fairs!

AS THINGS PICK UP, WE ALSO START TO GET SOME CREW MEMBERS ON WITH US. THE ROAD FAMILY STARTS TO GROW.

— MIKE PALMER

DAN HEINS: There's county fairs and there's state fairs. If you're doing county fairs, it can be pretty rough, depending on which part of the country you're in. We did a lot of them that first summer. I want to say it was close to 180 different fair dates we did, almost that entire year. California, Pennsylvania, Texas, Nebraska, Minneapolis. State fairs are usually bigger deals. Big stage, big PA, lots of people. But county fairs can be on hay wagons. We did one in, I think, Whitneyville, Pennsylvania, where we set up on two hay wagons, no lighting rig. We played before the sun went down, just had a little PA. It was so cool because usually there's catering, but they didn't have catering at this place. Local people baked and brought homemade food for us from their homes. It was good.

DAVE BUTZLER: We'd be doing county fairs, state fairs, we'd be at the pig hollering contest, and he'd show up. He'd take any kind of work. I came on to do lights, but you never knew what you'd get for lights at some shows, and we all always did whatever needed to be done.

The fairs are full of people like the ones we grew up with. **THEY WERE US.** -g

BRIAN PETREE: Back in the day we would call them the mud and dust tours.

G: A fair is a chance to see people in their own backyards. It's different from a club. At a fair you get to see the families. It's everybody that makes up that community, all different ages, and people who may be there for the goats and just happen to catch the show. It's usually outdoors, and here's the cool part: You're up against a thousand names that have played that fair in the past. So, you've got a chance to not only steal the show, but steal the show from ten years ago! This audience will remember. And if they like it, they're going to see you after the fair, meet the band, get something signed. They'll see all of what you stand for. And that's kind of like our bread and butter right there. The fairs are full of people like the ones we grew up with. They were us.

DAVE GANT: There was a guy from Zanesville, Ohio, named George Moffett. Still working, I think. He was the fair buyer, and we did a showcase in Nashville around fall of '89 for people who buy talent for fairs. He just loved what he saw in Garth, loved the energy. He loved the whole thing . . . including the cost. George Moffett buys 110 days of Garth. So, we ended up doing every little fair in Ohio. Ohio, West Virginia, Indiana.

G: Fairs were also fabulous because they'd put in their bids before things blew up for us. They were getting us at a rate that they couldn't have touched us for at that point. So, they're expecting us to come in with an attitude. But there we are, a bunch of boys from the Midwest, just looking for the sandwiches. It catches everybody off guard and it's not planned. *(laughs)* We still just felt fucking lucky that somebody wanted to come show up and hear us sing. I mean, I'm not going to tell you that we were just a bunch of humble kids. No, I definitely had my times when my ego is writing checks that my talent and my body can't cash. I'm not going to say it never got that way, but we loved it when the promoters or the fair people would look at us, chewing on our sandwiches, and go, "You guys don't have a clue who you are, do you?" You know? We all came from parents who would kick our ass if we said, "Fuck you, we sure do know who we are." We were all raised that way. And we all knew that this could be over in a heartbeat, so we were just enjoying it.

DAVE GANT: By the time we're halfway finished with those fairs, Garth was definitely a five figure act, middle five figures act by then. But the deal had been done before that happened—and Garth made good on every deal he agreed to. I remember we showed up to some of those fairs and . . . I swear, one of them we showed up and there was a Shure Vocal Master PA and three bug lights on a flatbed truck. *(laughs)* And there was John McBride, who was out on tour with us as production manager, saying, "Garth, do I have to get off the bus? Don't make me get off the bus." *(laughs)*

TRISHA YEARWOOD: Doing the fair circuit was like getting to be a part of a circus. So much fun. When I was opening shows for Garth, you'd get there in the morning, watch his sound check, do your own sound check, then be free to go on the rides, eat funnel cake. It was like being a kid every single night, all over the country. And a lot of these fairs were in small towns. You'd play in a field somewhere out on a race track or horse arena, might be in a town of 12,000 people, but for that week, when the fair's in town, there's 30,000 people a day. There's an excitement. Garth would have them pull the semis to the side and put the loading ramps off of the back of the trucks so that he could run up the ramps onto the truck or on top of the speakers. I can't even imagine what the safety codes were for that, but he wanted more room to run. You never saw a show like that . . . never . . . anywhere.

G: It didn't matter whether the production was a little shaky or not, it could be on the back of trucks. It didn't matter because at some point we're going to end up in the crowd anyway. We're going to be standing on speakers, even if they're about to fall off a flatbed truck. And I wouldn't trade those times for anything you might have to offer!

"IT WAS LIKE BEING A KID EVERY SINGLE NIGHT, ALL OVER THE COUNTRY."

- TRISHA YEARWOOD

In 1989, Nintendo introduced its first Game Boy, a handheld gaming device, causing a generation of parents to wonder where their children went. Milli Vanilli released an album that would win them a 1990 Grammy for Best New Artist, which they'd lose when it was discovered that the artists going under the name Milli Vanilli hadn't performed on their own recording. Tim Burton's dystopian fantasy *Batman* grossed over $400 million. As reality was challenged, replaced, and augmented, it was hard to say where one stood in this shifting world. Another film, *Field of Dreams,* suggested that people were searching to find an answer amidst it all. In the middle of such a moment, country music had a special place. Nashville music makers seemed to realize that, if you build it, they will come.

"Three chords and the truth." That was how Harlan Howard described what he felt was good country music. From Jimmie Rodgers to Hank Williams, country has been a source of emotional truth that has proved an anchor in changing times. In 1989, it was no different. Country music was bringing its listeners something they held close to their hearts.

5

AN OPENING ACT

1989–91

In country, rock, R&B, or any other genre, if you want a career, you need to get out on the road. And one of the best ways to do it is as an opening act. The Beatles did it, Prince did it, Dolly Parton did it. It was common sense in 1960, just as it was in 1989 and 1990, as Garth Brooks was on the cusp of an unprecedented career. Given the early signs of what was coming and the quality of his music, Brooks was offered some of the very best opening spots available. Kenny Rogers, The Judds, Reba: They all welcomed him onto their stages.

But what also happened that year for Garth Brooks came in the form of a succession of radio hits. "Much Too Young (To Feel This Damn Old)" led into "If Tomorrow Never Comes," "Not Counting You," and "The Dance." All made the top ten, including two number ones. For the headliners bringing Garth Brooks on tour, it was quickly generating a response beyond what was expected of an opening act.

HERE'S THE BEAUTIFUL THING
. . . class is always in session. And if you're out there fronting for other acts, well, that's the university. -g

G: You kind of knew clubs in and out. Because the club in North Carolina is not that different from the club in Wyoming in the sense that it's people just wanting to have a good time. You've got to find out if they're more of a cowboy crowd, more of a traditional country crowd, or if they are leaning on the modern side of country. But you *can* find that out. And we were covering all those bases, and having a hell of a time doing it. But then more and more opening spots started coming along.

BOB DOYLE: The opening spots were important in building this artist.

BEN FARRELL: Garth started with occasional opening spots, before the tours started coming. I eventually became his exclusive promoter. He opened for George Strait, who I worked with and who was one of Garth's idols, in Jackson, Mississippi, and Lafayette, Louisiana. These were strongholds for Strait, really hot places. Garth met him for the first time, I believe, in Jackson. And after meeting him, Garth is out there on his bus, and I'm on the bus with him. Garth says, "I know everything George Strait does is in-house." Now, I'd been working with Strait for years by that time, and Garth knew this. But Garth wants to learn everything he can from these guys, whether about the music or the business, just all of it. Garth says, "He's got you, he's got his manager, really controls his own destiny. But, man, this is going pretty far, Ben. I can't believe he's doing his own catering." I said, "What?" He said, "That truck down there." He points to a truck that has "George's Catering" written on the side. I'm like, "Garth, that's not George Strait . . . that's from George's Restaurant up the street!"

DAVE GANT: The opening spots were just sprinkled in. We were doing fairs, clubs, anything that would come our way. But, early on, we went out on a three-day weekend where it was Garth, Clint Black, and Ricky Van Shelton. The first gig was in Stillwater. That's where Garth went to college, that's Garth's turf.

G: I can't tell you what it's like to come back to where you came from, and you're on a stage opening for national acts, with a record of your own and a song on the radio. It may be that it never gets better than that . . . and it doesn't need to. That's a moment that just grabs you by the heart.

TY ENGLAND: Ricky was the headliner. He was entertainer of the year that year, I think, and Clint was having chart success, and then there was us. We were opening for everybody.

I can't tell you what it's like to
COME BACK TO WHERE YOU CAME FROM,
and you're on a stage opening for national acts. -g

DAN HEINS: I was still working for John McBride at that time. And John provided the PA for these three concerts. Garth Brooks was the opening act. At that time, none of us knew who Garth Brooks was. He had one song on the radio, "Much Too Young," but I'll tell you, we learned quickly who Garth Brooks was. He was the first act on the bill, but Garth kind of stole the show. He was a fireball onstage, came out, real personable guy. Everybody liked him. I don't think Garth's ever met anybody where that person didn't walk away from that meeting thinking they had a new best friend.

DAVE GANT: We had our six-song show together pretty well. It was tight. So, we get up there, and here's Stillwater, Garth's stomping grounds.

"EVERYBODY LIKED HIM.

I don't think Garth's ever met anybody where
that person didn't walk away
from that meeting thinking they had

A NEW BEST FRIEND."

- DAN HEINS

MIKE PALMER: At a certain point, everybody with an instrument would jump right off the stage and run around and play and come back up. It wasn't what country audiences were used to so much.

TY ENGLAND: So, we come to the climax of the show, and me and James look at each other. Now, at this point in time, we've got wireless guitars, and what we'd found playing at a lot of the honky-tonks was that if we'd get off the stage and into the audience, the crowd loved it. We didn't have in-ear monitors yet, so we couldn't hear shit out there, but it didn't matter. So, on this show, we make eye contact, and we're going to run and jump off the stage . . . except this stage was like 16 feet high. My heel still hurts to this day. I think that might have been the last stage I jumped off without checking first. Anyway, we ran out in the crowd and came back, climbed up the front of the stage and finished the show. The crowd is roaring, standing on their tippy toes.

DAVE GANT: You would have thought it was the Beatles. This place was going nuts. Hometown boy does good, right? Dan Heins was working for the sound company, and that's when Garth offered Dan the job to be our house sound guy, after those three shows. Dan's been with us ever since.

G: Then I get the call from Bob Doyle saying that Kenny Rogers is going to the Northeast and wants us on the tour.

BOB DOYLE: Kenny Rogers was already successful in places we hadn't gotten to. In Texas the club circuit was happening in a big way, but Garth wasn't yet a national phenomenon.

G: I said, Kenny Rogers! Man, Kenny Rogers came from The First Edition. I knew him as pop. Then he got into country and just took off there, too. Bob said to me, "They're not going to let someone that looks like you and sounds like you in the Northeast this early in your career. This guy owns the Northeast and he's offering the slot to you." Bob says, "*Take it*. Take it, take it, take it." And in one city at a time in the Northeast, we'd get a chance to be in front of these people, Kenny's people. We took it.

DAVE GANT: Kenny Rogers' Christmas tour was a big deal. It was mainly all Northeast. That was another jumping step for Garth.

G: The second you meet Kenny Rogers, you fall in love with him. He is a people person. And as an entertainer, sorry, it doesn't get better. He brought us on this Christmas tour in the Northeast, 1989. This guy was sincere. Watching this man, I really learned about how to treat people. If anybody ever says to me, "Man, you take your time with people, where did you get that?" I'll tell them right away, Kenny Rogers. One of the sweetest men ever, and he takes time for everybody.

BOB DOYLE: Garth has always been Garth. But I think Kenny Rogers showed him that even on a big tour, with lots of personnel and crew, with all that work to do, you could keep being your best and treat people right. It was a great first tour to get on.

TRISHA YEARWOOD: Well, I can tell you that there is not a better just observer and a sponge than Garth. He'd be a great detective because he notices everything. He's that guy, detail oriented, notices and learns and studies. He wants to learn. With Kenny Rogers it was like Entertaining 101. I also did a Christmas tour with Kenny, and he had an ability to communicate with his audience that made you feel so connected to him. I think that's something that Garth does incredibly well. I've been to Garth shows where I go out in the arena and stand all the way in the back just to see it. He'd be singing some song, and I'd be like, *Oh my gosh, I think he sees me.* But he does that to every single person in the arena. That's something that Kenny Rogers did.

G: When you're in clubs, you judge your success by how packed that floor is. We were raised to understand that if those people aren't dancing, then they ain't digging what you're doing, and if the bar guys aren't selling any beer, then you ain't gonna be called back. So, in clubs, we got that whole place hopping, and what we'd hear from the owner every night was, "Holy shit, boys, we set a record in beer sales!" Now we go to arenas, what are we going to do? Seats everywhere and nobody's dancing. You could hear a pin drop while you're playing, but, if you did it right, you'd have to hold your ears because they're so loud after that song. Kenny Rogers did this unbelievably well. So, yeah, you're going to school. You're watching how he's working an arena, and I'm loving every second of it.

DAN HEINS: Garth had those people in the palm of his hand, and that's when it really became evident to me that this guy really has no problem communicating to a small or large audience. Kenny Rogers' crowd was a lot more reserved than the bars, you know, they weren't as fanatical, but he would just find the way to communicate with them. I remember Kenny's production manager just like in awe of Garth's command of the stage. I think the comment was, "It's like throwing a duck into water." It was that natural for him just to walk out there, not nervous and he's kind of this new, upcoming artist. Kenny's this veteran superstar that had seen and done everything. But Garth didn't have any of those rough edges that you see with new artists sometimes when they're trying too hard. With Garth, it would just flow out.

LANNY LANDERS: I spent about twenty-five years on the Kenny Rogers tour before working on Garth's crew. And I remember when he was an opening act for Kenny. I can't remember exactly how long, but several weeks. He was new to me, you know, because it was early in his career. It was real straight-ahead country and he was real impressive. I thought he was great. He just struck me as someone who was real, if that makes any sense. I mean, you can kind of get the feeling whether somebody is truly good, or if they're just up there trying to make a buck. I could see something special up there.

DAVE GANT: The first show of the Kenny tour was in Cape Girardeau, Missouri, and it wound back to the Northeast after that. It was Garth, Eddie Rabbitt, and Kenny Rogers. We're all getting ready to go play "If Tomorrow Never Comes," and we're barely into the song, right about where the band just comes in, and . . . Garth breaks down, right there onstage.

G: Really, we're going to tell this one?

The second you meet Kenny Rogers,
YOU FALL IN LOVE WITH HIM. -g

LANNY LANDERS: That kind of emotion is not something that people do onstage. He just really stopped and broke down, if I remember correctly. And he said something about infidelity and that he felt like hell. I don't remember exactly what got said, but it was really sincere and it just shocked the hell out of me.

MIKE PALMER: Well, Garth never worked from a script. But if ever there was one, this definitely wasn't on it.

G: Somehow we'd been double-booked. And I had to get on this flight, one of those little prop planes, just me and Tim Bowers. We both saw it, that, yeah, we were dead. We really thought the plane was going to crash, and as soon as I hit the ground I went to a pay phone, called Sandy and said, "Look, I just went through one of the most horrific experiences of my life and all I could think of was . . . I need to clear things with you." And, so I did, I needed to tell her. Then we had to go on the stage, and I get to "If Tomorrow Never Comes" and . . . and I just lost it.

MIKE PALMER: I'm just thinking, *Keep playing, keep playing . . . don't do this Garth. We're all going to be out of a job. Don't do this.* So, I keep playing, just holding down a beat.

G: I stopped the song, right? But the drums, the drums are the only thing that doesn't stop. I look back, and Palmer has his head straight up, his face, tears are coming out of his eyes, and he's shaking his head like, *Don't stop, don't stop, don't do what you're about to do.*

I'm just thinking,

KEEP PLAYING, KEEP PLAYING . . .

- MIKE PALMER

DAVE GANT: I'm looking at Palmer, and you could hear a pin drop it was so quiet, and Garth is crying, saying he's sorry, asking for another chance. I'd never seen anything like this.

BOB DOYLE: It made me realize, okay, this is a guy who's not going to lie, he's always going to tell the truth, come what may. I don't know what inspired him to reveal it like he did, but, on the other hand, here he is with his fans, just being honest about a situation as a human being and the frailties that we all have. But, yeah, I remember it. It was like, *okay. . . (laughs) now what?* But had it been revealed as a sort of tabloid thing, in another way, it would have been totally different and *received* totally differently.

LANNY LANDERS: He kind of stopped and broke down onstage. You know, I think he started to cry, and I was standing with a couple people I worked with on Kenny's crew, and we felt like, *well, this is strange*, you know? *What is this about?* Now that I've known Garth for quite a while, I realize that he is the least filtered, hiding-behind-a-persona guy you'd ever want to meet. I mean he is Garth. He's himself. And this was my first experience of it.

TY ENGLAND: The announcement to the crowd was Garth saying how he had just let somebody down, somebody that he cared about, and how hurt he felt to have done it. It was really a tough moment. And I think for all of us there was a shadow of doubt, like, *Hey, what happens now?* But, finally, I saw that it was endearing to the crowd, to see somebody be real. And we were real. We were never the guys that sang off a sheet. Not with Garth. Everything we did was at an emotional level. Every song we sang. Every time we played "The Dance."

G: Looking back now, would I have done it that way again? I don't know. When you wear your heart on your sleeve for a nation to see, that nation is going to find things that they love about you and they're going to find things that they don't like about you. And here it came. So much support from that crowd, it was deafening and so uplifting at the time.

AFTER THAT, WE PLAYED BIGGER AND BIGGER VENUES, AND WE PLAYED WITH MORE AND MORE ARTISTS. GARTH OPENED FOR REBA, FOR THE JUDDS, AND WE JUST GOT MORE AND MORE EXPERIENCE WITH LARGER AND LARGER CROWDS.

– TY ENGLAND

DAVE GANT: I remember going back to the hotel afterwards and Eddie Rabbitt walks up to me and goes, "Does he always do that?" No, I tell him. "Well, he should," he says. *(laughs)*

DAN HEINS: In the end, no one thought less of him for telling the truth. Just the opposite.

G: Not the response I was anticipating . . . thank God.

TY ENGLAND: After Kenny, we played bigger and bigger venues, and we played with more and more artists. Garth opened for Reba, for The Judds, and we just got more and more experience with larger and larger crowds. We traveled three hundred and some days the first year. We'd mostly sleep on the bus, and we'd get two hotel rooms to shower and clean up. Sometimes everybody had already been in the shower when I got there, and there's one wash rag left to dry off with. It was a hard road that first year, pretty grueling, but we were really picking up steam.

G: So, let's say you get to graduate from the Kenny Rogers school of entertainment. Now, get ready to go to the next level: the Reba McEntire tour. Nobody works harder. Nobody puts in more hours than Reba. She's so Oklahoma, of course, she's a goddess to me. Reba was the one that made it from Oklahoma. She's also a female, and you watch her run her ship as good, if not better, than any male. Her people love her. Down-home sincerity, unbelievable voice, the production is immaculate. I'm just watching the pacing of the show now . . . how you take them from the big thrill of the introduction, hold onto them in the middle and then leave them at the end with something even bigger. This was good for me.

MIKE PALMER: We got on that tour, and Reba was a great human being. She had a really good show, too, running back to change costumes four, five, six times.

G: They say movies are hard on women. I can't imagine movies being harder on women than music is. They have to work a thousand times more to get a tenth as much. But, when you have people like Dolly Parton and Reba McEntire, that's what you're going to get. You're going to get women that never, ever stop working. Reba had that hands-on, eye-to-eye kind of connection to people, always having time for what's going on. And when you're lucky enough to be standing beside the stage when she's doing sound check, get ready. She's got a list of everything from the night before, and she doesn't just talk to the band leader and the band leader talks to everybody else. She's calling them all out, same way with Dolly. Dolly calls everyone out, individually, "Let's do this here, let's do this here. What do you think?" Beautiful.

TY ENGLAND: I think we were all learning something, every time we got on another bill as opener. You'd have to close your eyes if you *didn't* want to learn. We were out there with the best.

G: Then here comes the last fronting thing, and it's The Judds' farewell tour. As big a deal as you're going to get in country music. It was their final run, and it was emotional, for the band, for the crew, and for those two remarkable women. For them, everyone was at the end of something, and not everyone was sure what was coming next. How could it not be emotional? And, for us, we are at the door of . . . just an explosion with our career. It was a kind of beginning. Every opening act that is going to go on gets to that point where they have grown beyond the opening slot. And that's where we were. Remember, these things are all booked way in advance, before anyone knew what was coming. We were fronting what has to be the most successful duo in country music history, but we were building so fast ourselves. We knew this was the last front gig. But if it was going to be anyone, Miss Naomi and Miss Wynonna were the ones to be with. Remarkable performers. Just being out there with them on their last tour, we were a part of history.

I did a lot of tours with other artists, all wonderful,

BUT THIS WAS LIKE GETTING TO OPEN FOR ELVIS.

- TRISHA YEARWOOD

DAVE GANT: I remember Garth had a bunch of dates he had to cancel because of that Kenny Rogers tour. What he did was tell all the club owners that he'd come back the next year at the same money they booked him for originally. By the time he did those shows, though, Garth had four singles and was one of the biggest things in country music. We'd go in these clubs the next year where you couldn't even breathe, you know, because Garth's here, and they were packed beyond capacity.

MARK GREENWOOD: 1991 was an odd year in the sense that it was a really strange hodgepodge of gigs. It could go from opening for The Judds to doing a county fair to headlining a gig as big as The Judds' shows to doing a club, because Garth promised he'd come back and always made good on those promises. It was strange, but it was great because there was this feeling of things taking off. But pretty soon, it's Garth who has the openers, like a torch is being passed. And the first time we have our own opener, I think it's . . .

G: Trisha Yearwood. Who else could it be?

TRISHA YEARWOOD: There was that great meeting with Garth and my label head, Tony Brown, where Garth offered to take me on tour. By that time Garth Brooks was the biggest thing ever, so everybody wanted to be on that tour. The fact that I got that opportunity was incredible. It was like getting to be in on the beginning of the big, big phenomenon that was Garth Brooks. I did a lot of tours with other artists, all wonderful, but this was like getting to open for Elvis.

G: But, you know, it's your first time headlining a tour, and you look out at sound check and . . . that's a lot of fucking seats. *(laughs)* And when they're empty, it looks like there are a lot more, so you go, *Man, I just hope somebody shows up!* The first gig is in Indianapolis, at Deer Creek. You do sound check, and then you make sure that opening act gets treated the way Kenny Rogers and Reba McEntire treated theirs, right?

You know, it's your first time headlining a tour, and you look out at sound check and . . .

THAT'S A LOT OF FUCKING SEATS. -g

JOHNNY GARCIA: The first show we did was in Indianapolis, June of '91 at a place called Deer Creek. When we pulled in there in the afternoon, Garth came over to our bus—it was Trisha, the band, and a couple of crew guys that we had, all on the same bus. We opened the door, and he greeted every one of us, and he's like, "You're on a Garth Brooks tour. Whatever you need, just talk to us. We're here for you." It was amazing from day one.

G: Here comes the opening act, and it's easily 100 degrees at this point, and she's wearing a black felt jacket. I look at her and I go, "Are you sure this is what you want to wear on this show?" *(laughs)* She goes, "It's the only thing I brought." I said, "Okay, but, look, everything from those stage wings out there left and right, it's all yours. Just go have fun, do it." And she said, "I would rather not. I just want to kind of stand right here." *(laughs)* I said, "Okay, whatever makes you comfortable, but you are, you're going to kill them tonight." And, my God, she did. It was awesome. It was fun, the whole show was fun. And we went out and signed autographs together afterward. There were people as far as you could see. We probably did a year with Trisha. That was her first ever opening gig, it was our first ever having an opening act.

MIKE PALMER: It was pretty much all arenas from that point forward.

G: In the summer of '91, we're playing Scottsdale, Arizona, playing the Quarter Horse Show there. It's easily 115 degrees, and it's outdoors. You just stay on the air-conditioned bus. We were going on in the evening, but they have acts going on throughout the day. When Trisha goes on, you know you're next. Of course, it was John McBride's sound company. He's losing amp after amp in this heat. This is his life savings invested in this sound company. I look out of the bus, and there's a little girl that looks like she is five foot tall, maybe a hundred pounds, dragging these hundred-pound bags of ice and stacking them around the amplifiers, trying to keep them cool. My brother Kelly is standing right next to me, and I go, "Wow, who's that?" He goes, "That's John McBride's wife." I said, "Well, damn, she's a hard worker." And Kelly goes, "You know, she sings."

JOHN MCBRIDE: Martina got signed in '91. Around the time she was making her first record, Garth called up and said, "Hey, what are you guys doing tonight? Come by." So, we went by his house and we were sitting out there and just talking and hanging out and he asked Martina how the record was going. She goes, "Oh, great." He goes, "Well, what's it like, can you sing anything?" And she sang part of a song called "When You Are Old," not one that was ever a single or anything but a beautiful song with great words. And Garth's a lyric guy, too. So, she sang part of the song, and the first thing he says is, "Well, that record ought to be cheap to make, because you don't really need a band." He was being complimentary of her voice, of course. Then he said, "Hey, Martina, I got a favor to ask, would you mind opening my tour next year?" And she said, *"Well let me think about, okay I will."* Not a second's pause. *(laughs)* She opened all eighty or so shows or whatever we did in '92. And she got to see him onstage and, well, you learn. You learn, you see how it is and what works and what doesn't. We had a great time.

G: It was a chance for man and wife to be together. Having Martina as an opening act also made me look brilliant as I was given the credit for her talent. And her talent was amazing. Being a part of that chain is one of the greatest things that can happen to an artist. So, I was a headliner now . . . but not for one second did that mean my lessons were over. Hardly. Class was just getting started.

It's not every performer who outgrows the opening spot in a short period of time, but Garth Brooks was one such entertainer.

By the time he'd finished touring with The Judds, the industry could see that this was an artist ready to headline. The word-of-mouth among fans regarding his live shows, the support from radio, and Brooks' eagerness to spend time getting to know his fans: It all fueled his quick ascent to the top of the country music charts. And that may have been what many viewed as the highest peak a country artist could hit while still being country.

Historically, there had been artists associated with country, among them Dolly Parton, Glen Campbell, Roger Miller, Skeeter Davis, even Patsy Cline, who experienced crossover success either by exploring pop material or by sheer good fortune with a particular cut. Pop audiences were no strangers to the sound of country. It was infectious. Even over there on pop radio. The country sound came through in recordings from Billy Swan's "I Can Help" to Jeannie C. Riley's "Harper Valley P.T.A." and B.J. Thomas' "Another Somebody Done Somebody Wrong Song." But there wasn't a lot of evidence that a country artist could cross over doing traditional country and stay over for more than the time it took to have a hit single. The Beatles let Ringo sing "Act Naturally," a Buck Owens song, because they loved country music. And their audience was happy for it, but the group always got back to the material they were best known for. So, if you looked at the past, it made no sense to think that a country artist could make a home on the pop charts. Not without leaving their cowboy hat at home. But that was all about to change. For the first time ever.

(6) HEADLINER!

1990–94

By the time Garth Brooks started headlining his own shows, no one was describing him as "one of the hat acts." He was no longer put into a category, because he'd become his own category. In country music circles, his success was the best news anyone could get. Garth was an emblem of the possibilities. And outside of country music, there was a new awareness of a genre that had too often been left out of view. But it wasn't just a victory for country music, it was a victory for the many country fans who felt like they were a part of an unseen America. Garth's visibility was, somehow, a thing they participated in. The headlining tours would be a victory lap for all, and the best party to pull into town in a long, long time.

There's something about walking out on that stage, knowing that this is *your* audience. You don't need to win them over . . . you just need to

GIVE THEM THE BEST NIGHT YOU CAN POSSIBLY GIVE THEM.

-g

TRISHA YEARWOOD: You don't get into this *not* wanting to headline your own tour. That's the dream you come in with. Then . . . then the anxiety of being the person who is responsible for putting butts in seats, selling those tickets, being the headliner, that kicks in, and it's real.

JOHN MCBRIDE: As early as the fall of '90, Garth started taking off like a bat out of hell. I always attributed it to his live show. That was number one. Couldn't have happened without great songs and great records—but he had that covered in spades. I just remember when I came back from those first three shows where Garth opened for Ricky Van Shelton. Martina heard me going on and on and on about this Garth Brooks guy who threw his hat around in the air and climbed up on the lighting rig, how amazing he was. And I wasn't alone. So, yeah, I really think it was his live show that made him a star.

MIKE PALMER: I remember my dad taking me to see the three-ring circus, and by the time it's all over, there was so much going on, I was just so exhausted, falling asleep on the way out. I think that a lot of what we do up there is like that. Everyone's on the move, covering every side of the stage. Jimmy Mattingly's running around, I'm running around, Johnny's back and forth and so, the singers. We're trying to keep up with Garth's energy. And that's what he's always wanted.

DAVE GANT: *Garth Brooks, No Fences, Ropin' the Wind*, those three albums. It was so wild, just took off exponentially. Boom! He's moved up. And then here's "Friends in Low Places." And despite all that, it took a little bit for Garth to get into the Opry. No one was quite sure what to do with this person.

G: The Opry is every guy's dream. Every country artist's dream, to get that call. We had "Much Too Young" and "If Tomorrow Never Comes." We get a second number one with "Not Counting You." Now it's "The Dance," "Friends in Low Places," and still no call from the Opry. I got to tell you, there's been that thing about not being the industry's darling. I kind of feel like, "Oh crap, what have I done? Or what do I need to do?" Then I get the sweetest call from Bob Doyle. He goes, "Hey, you're not going to believe it, but Hal Durham from the Opry wants us to come out and talk to him." So, Bob and I get in the truck to go out and talk to him. Sweetest guy on the planet. He goes, "I'm going to start this conversation by telling you I owe you an apology." I thought, *What does this guy owe me an apology for?* He says, "We wanted you on here about eight months ago, but we saw your show and we were worried that you had a drug problem." *(laughs)*

Nobody had ever put that much energy into live country music. GARTH WAS SOMETHING NEW ... and not everyone knew what to make of it. - DAN HEINS

DAN HEINS: Nobody had ever put that much energy into live country music. Garth was something new . . . and not everyone knew what to make of it.

G: Getting to be a member of the Grand Ole Opry is just . . . it's a thing that never goes away, just beautiful. When people ask what the highlight of my career is, I say being a member of the Grand Ole Opry. Look at that family. Just being a part of that family.

BEN FARRELL: He'd been waiting for his moment to go out there and be Garth Brooks. He knew what that was all about. And the moment had come. When we played the Calgary Stampede, 360,000 people tried to buy a ticket for one show.

G: When we became headliners, there were two things to think about: First, how can we make this different from what we've done before, and, second, how can we keep what we've got, even if the rooms are getting bigger.

DAN HEINS: When I first saw Garth, it was when people were having big '80s hair and, you know, country artists were trying to be more of a pop thing. Then he came out with his Wranglers and his Ropers. He just touched people. He was always picking songs or writing songs that . . . I mean, he would never do a song that he didn't have some heartfelt connection to. If it wasn't going to communicate or touch somebody deep and directly, for him it probably wasn't worth doing.

G: We were playing Bull Run, a huge show, when Tim Bowers steps on some cable that knocks everything out. I still had my guitar and vocal working, but we lost everything else. So, in the middle of the show I went back to just guitar and vocal, until they got everything up and running. I may as well have been back at Willie's. But then you saw how well it worked. The audience just pulled in around it, started singing with me. From that moment forward, that stays in the show. I could do "Unanswered Prayers" or something just with the people singing. Something happens when the audience gets to hear themselves. They know what they sound like, and it's fabulous. Suddenly they're not watching a show . . . they're in one. And once you get them there, you've found a way for them to sing all night long, where it feels like they are as much of the show as the band is.

DAVE BUTZLER: Garth knew how to bring the audience in close and create a kind of intimate feeling in a big venue. Not easy to do. But that was just one side of a show. He also wanted the big side, you know? When I first met him, he was like, "What are your favorite bands?" We were just kind of talking. I say, Kiss and Queen. "Oh, yeah? Me, too." He said he'd love to some day have a big system like that, and I'm thinking that would be pretty cool. Then it happened. And it was great because he would never tell me that there was a budget I had to stick to. The conversation was all about, "What does the show need?" That's always where we started. So, I could dream a little. He was always my lighting sugar daddy. He'd laugh when I called him that, but I meant it.

G: I see Janet Jackson wearing a headset. And I see Wynonna wearing a headset. So I say to the crew, I'm like, "Guys, where do these things come from?" They introduce me to some guys at a company called Crown, and I sit and talk to them. I said, "I'm going to need to get one of these, but I don't want to drag a wire around the stage." They go, "No, no, no, we've got you covered." I said, "Well, I'll still have to drag a wire on my guitar." They said, "No, no, no, we got you covered." Totally wireless, guitar and mic. Suddenly the stage opened up like never before. No more leash. It changed the show.

DAVE GANT: Ultimate mobility is what I think he was after, what I'm *sure* he was after. It had to be '92, '93 that Crown was out at every show for about six months. We had two Crown guys out, and they would listen and work and then come back, "Try this." At the time there weren't good headset microphones. You could get either durability or tone, but you couldn't have both. They figured that out for Garth . . . and we never saw him again! *(laughs)* He was on the move.

"When people ask what
the highlight of my career is,
I say being a member of
THE GRAND OLE
OPRY. LOOK AT
THAT FAMILY. JUST
BEING PART OF
THAT FAMILY."

- g

G: Now I was in that space between the band and the audience, the best place to be. Now it was just easier to feel what was needed. Every audience is different, and things happen that are unplanned, that you need to react to spontaneously. That's the excitement of the live thing, right there.

DAVE BUTZLER: That's been one thing about being around him, it's always been fun. Of course, once the children started coming, everybody tried to calm him down because he used to climb up on the truss and focus the lights for me when we were doing fair dates and stuff. He just loved climbing around on the ladders and stuff like that. He wasn't scared of that at all, but he'd go up, and we'd get half of it done, and then he'd have to come down and go do a radio interview or something. But that guy you see in the show, he's still there afterwards, there before. He's that guy.

JIMMY MATTINGLY: He will change it up on you. Everybody knows. You get a set list, but that doesn't really mean anything. If he doesn't feel like something is right or if he thinks something could be better than what he had planned, he'll just switch it. And hopefully we'll all be watching and we'll know. You got to read him, figure out where you think he wants the band out for a song, or if he wants just himself. Recently we came to the end of a show, and the whole band had left. They were heading down the hallway and going to the van. I noticed that he didn't look like he was gonna leave. So I waited. He decided to do a song called "Wild Horses," which is usually the whole band. He says, "We'll do 'Wild Horses.' Hey, Jimmy, you want to come and play this with me?" I'm thinking, *Now how does he know I'm the only guy standing down here?*

DAVE BUTZLER: He's never done a set list song to song. Somewhere along the line, it's going to be different. I think he does a lot of that on purpose, because he wants every concert to be different somehow and he wants that energy. As the lighting guy, I just focus on him 100 percent. Sometimes he'll go off into a song we've never heard, so you got to just follow him.

G: The wireless world coincided with bigger, more interesting stages. And we're all getting into working that space. And I'm telling you, this is as much fun as a person can have.

JOHNNY GARCIA: He wants us all to be entertainers without ever really telling us that. If you look at every band member up there, that's what they are, you know. Sometimes he'll even say before the show, "Get up there and kick my ass. Steal my thunder." He loves it.

G: I put a $500 bounty on my own head. Any crew or band guy that could knock me on my ass during the show would get $500. I was trying anything. And the band had fun with it. You remember this stuff for the rest of your life. Debbie Nims was out with us, and she needed the money worse than anybody. She had a kid and just needed it, so she hit me three times during the show. Tried to knock me down, and she weighs about a hundred pounds. It was like, *Debbie, all right . . .* so finally, at the end of the night, we did the bow and they all just piled on top of me and took me down, so everybody split the $500.

MIKE PALMER: Yeah. Our steel guitar player Steve McClure used to say, "This ain't music, this is hockey." He was a steel player, but even when he'd play guitar he would try to stay in his area, and Garth would come up and bodycheck him. Everyone was bouncing off each other. That was part of the fun.

TY ENGLAND: Garth and I would do "Two of a Kind" and run around, chasing each other around the stage. At that time we had this big horseshoe-shaped stage. And we would start on the flat ground and run up the ramps and meet each other at the back of the horseshoe, parting ways, with me going to sing at one side and Garth on the other. I was in position but look over and, out of the corner of my eye, I see James kind of wincing and looking at me like something is about to happen. I kind of turned my head and I see Garth running around this horseshoe and just at the top of the ramp he leaps . . . *and he's trying to jump all of the way over me standing up.* But he wasn't running fast enough. I felt a boot hit me about mid-back, and he pressed me to the stage. I went all the way to the floor and became a bit of a step stool for Garth that night. This was a Garth show. You got a few bumps and bruises in the name of entertainment.

G: Each time we take a step forward, get used to bigger venues, a new challenge comes. And I loved it. The stadiums were exactly that, you know? We'd figured out how to reach five hundred people in a club, twelve thousand in an arena . . . but eighty thousand? Willie's didn't train me for that. Houston Livestock and Rodeo was in '93, and it was something altogether new.

MIKE PALMER: The Astrodome was a mess to begin with because of the echo. We were right in the middle, underneath the dome, and there was a lot of delay, with sounds bouncing off the dome and coming back a few seconds later. We were all wearing in-ear monitors by then, but Garth didn't like them because he felt like he couldn't hear the audience as well as he wanted to. He didn't want to lose that connection.

G: They're going to pull the stage out into the middle of the Astrodome when it's showtime, if you can imagine that.

MARK GREENWOOD: I was on the crew at the time, and the first thing that comes to mind is that it was the worst sounding venue we'd ever been in. The reverb goes on forever and *(laughs)* they basically haul you out—on a stage with everything set up!—over to the riding area. It's really bumpy. You're holding onto drum cymbal stands and things so that they don't fall over.

"Every audience is different, and things happen that are unplanned, that you need to react to spontaneously.

THAT'S THE EXCITEMENT OF THE LIVE THING, RIGHT THERE."

- g

G: Now, everything that isn't in the stands is dirt. It's a rodeo. They're pulling this stage into the middle of just . . . acres of dirt. There's all this space between us and the audience, and I'm wondering how you get people out on the field. Then I find out that the plan is this: There won't be any people out on the field. I'm thinking, *So, you're telling me you're going to drive me out on a flatbed trailer into the middle of this thing, and the nearest person is going to be seventy yards away from me in all directions? Yes. What the fuck is this?* How do you . . . how do you reach the people? Surely they're not just going to sit there in their seats and go, *Hey, this is great, we get to see a guy sing songs from seventy yards away with nobody in between us and him.* Yeah. *(laughs)*

DAVE BUTZLER: Just another free-for-all. Garth jumped into the back of a truck and rode around, and everybody is wondering what in the hell is he doing. I'm like, *Well, he's going to say hi to everybody.* Next thing I know he's got the band convinced to jump off the stage and run over towards people to do solos and stuff. Was it scheduled, was it on my radar? No. But you've got a guitar player who just jumped off stage and is running all over, so, you better keep a spotlight on him. Baptism by fire. If you've never heard that phrase, it's one Garth uses a lot. *We'll get there, don't worry.*

Our steel guitar player Steve McClure used to say,
THIS AIN'T MUSIC, THIS IS HOCKEY.
- MIKE PALMER

G: The show's over, and we go back to playing places, but Houston Livestock and Rodeo kind of opened everything up for us, just out of necessity. We had to push out toward the audience just to connect, and it worked, and it was something that would work everywhere, you know? What made sense in a stadium applied everywhere. Go out there and meet your audience. Walk through whatever dirt and mud you need to, but meet them where they are.

BOB DOYLE: The rodeos we've played have been important to Garth. Houston Livestock and Rodeo, Calgary Stampede, definitely Cheyenne Frontier Days, particularly the 100th Anniversary with Chris LeDoux. Garth will always say he's not a cowboy, but I think there's something about the lifestyle, the culture, the athleticism, that he was drawn to and loved to sing about. He appreciated what it was and knew its place in American life. Every album has a cowboy song, "Rodeo," "The Cowboy Song," "Beaches of Cheyenne." It's also there in his admiration of Chris LeDoux. I think it's also that whole workingman sensibility. The cowboy is just as much a part of it as the steamfitter, the auto worker, whatever. They're real, and I think he sings to it.

TRACY GREENWOOD: Those are his fans, his core. Rodeo people. Growing up in Oklahoma, I think it was always a part of his culture. And Chris LeDoux was someone Garth respected so much, a big part of his world.

G: The 100th anniversary of the grandaddy of them all, Cheyenne Frontier Days! You're lucky just to get to play Cheyenne. It's the real deal. We'd played it a few times already, and these are real cowboys, no shit, just horses everywhere, tied up around the stage. It's awesome. It's fun and, damn it, you're part of the family here, like, *Come grab a paper plate, eat with the rest of us.* Everybody treats you like you're a cousin or something. Sweet people.

BAPTISM BY FIRE.
If you've never heard that phrase, it's one Garth uses a lot.
WE'LL GET THERE, DON'T WORRY.
- DAVE BUTZLER

MARK GREENWOOD: They had stagecoach races, bull riding and roping, barrel races, all this stuff that you would see at a typical rodeo. The difference is that the nighttime stuff gets really wild. There were people riding horses into bars in really nice hotels, just doing crazy stuff because it's Cheyenne Frontier Days and you can do that and get away with it.

G: I'm fired up, but I'm starting to look at the date on it, and I go, "Why does that date look familiar to me?" We couldn't have double-booked. Then, oh my God, that's our baby's due date. I don't know what to do here. So, Bob Doyle calls up Chris LeDoux and says, "Hey man, would you ever consider playing Cheyenne for us if we can't get there?" He says of course. So, we're in Cheyenne, loading in the day before. Everybody's waiting by their phones to see what happens. LeDoux shows up with his guys—day of the show—because he was playing the night before. Shows up about two in the afternoon. I get a call saying, "Hey, it looks like everything is going to be fine." She doesn't feel like the baby is going to be coming tonight, tells me to enjoy it then get home.

BRYAN KENNEDY: I'm just one of the guys that always wanted to be a cowboy. I am that Louis L'Amour-reading dreamer. Garth asked me to open the Cheyenne 100th, and it was a huge thrill for me. Cowboys . . . everywhere. And Chris LeDoux.

G: I go to Chris, "Hey, it looks like everything is going to be fine, and I can't thank you enough." I told him I want to pay him for bringing his guys all the way up there. He says, "No, no, no." I insist. He says no. Then I did the thing you don't do to cowboys. I reached out and touched him and said, "Really, please, let me just pay." And I shit you not, this guy looked at me, was just looking at me, and I was like, *Who is this guy? I've never seen him before.* He looked at me and goes, "No, and that's it." Silence. Okay. Stubborn as a damn mule. I said, "Got it, but can I ask you a favor then, since you're already here, will you come out and sing 'What You Gonna Do With a Cowboy' with me?" Cheyenne Frontier Days and you're singing with Chris LeDoux? They can't make a movie with that script that good. So, it's showtime and I go out there, and I feel like I'm kicking their asses all over the place. Then Chris LeDoux walks out, and that place goes fucking bananas. This guy walks out and this place is all his. It's like pouring gasoline on a fire.

JIMMY MATTINGLY: When we went to do Cheyenne it was, well, here's Garth, the cowboy that's on top of the world, coming to do the cowboy event of the world. It was huge. It was as big as big gets. And serious fun. I knew it was going to be good, then Chris LeDoux is added in. When you meet Chris LeDoux, he's really meek and sweet. It's like, "I don't get it." Then, when he comes up onstage, he just comes alive.

G: Everybody in the band is just kind of pinching themselves. His band, The Western Underground, is over there onstage right just smiling because they see this every night . . . but this is new territory for us, man. This guy walks out, and it's unbelievable. The reverence, the respect, the excitement in that crowd . . . and he's beautiful, too, man. Beautiful smile, perfect. If you could combine him and Strait, you'd get the guy I want to be, though I'll never be a tenth of either one of them. But it was really cool to be right there, to feel that electricity, feel that charge. Damn, that's someone to have as a mentor and a hero. Cheyenne 100th . . . I don't know how it gets bigger than that. This is what dreams are made of if you're a kid, and that's just what I am standing there watching this man. He was a good man.

BOB DOYLE: Once we get to the point where Garth's headlining, that band is having some experiences out there. They're going through something rare, something special. Of course, they're still a band.

TY ENGLAND: Okay, so we were up to absolutely no good. We would sometimes be going out of our minds. We had no satellite TV on the bus, no DVDs. Just a deck of cards and an impulse to find new ways to torture each other.

You're lucky just to get to play
Cheyenne. It's the real deal.

THESE ARE REAL COWBOYS, NO SHIT, JUST HORSES EVERYWHERE, TIED UP AROUND THE STAGE. IT'S AWESOME."

- g

"When you meet Chris LeDoux, he's really meek and sweet. It's like, 'I don't get it.' Then, **WHEN HE COME UP ONSTAGE, HE JUST COMES ALIVE."**

- JIMMY MATTINGLY

DAVE BUTZLER: Mike Palmer and some of the others were after the merchandise guy. The first time they came to me looking for a lug wrench and a jack, I knew there was something going on. They'd be jacking up the merch guys' van and making the wheels loose and stuff, so when they'd get in to leave the wheels would fall off and they'd realize they're up on cinder blocks. The bus would drive off and leave them.

MIKE PALMER: Well, Ty and I roomed together initially. And Steve McClure and James Garver shared a room. They were both from Kansas, knew each other back there and moved to Nashville. It was sort of us against those two for a little bit. Then it branched out. It picked up once we were doing our own shows. I remember when Restless Heart was opening at a festival. John Dittrich was the drummer, and I loved him to death. His drums were right in front of mine, which were up on a riser. I was able to crawl underneath and be screened off, so I could see them but they couldn't see me. While they were playing, I got up there with my spare snare. He's hitting the 2 and the 4, and I'd play just behind the beat a little bit so it'd sound like slapback, a confusing echo. Everyone would be freaking out, then I'd start going ahead of the beat. They're like, *How is this happening?!* I love that one.

TY ENGLAND: Steve McClure was just a little different than all of us. He had really dry humor and was a little bit diabolical somewhere on the inside. And he loved to pull pranks on people. One night he had some sort of a firecracker, and we found a way to sneak into Dave Gant's room while he was asleep. Steve put a fairly large firecracker under a tin can in the bathtub and lit it. Of course, the firecracker went off, smoked up the room, set the fire alarm off, and burnt a hole in the tub. That was like the worst we got. But that was kind of bad enough.

DAVE BUTZLER: We were down in, I think, Louisiana and Stephanie Davis put some goats in Garth's dressing room. He was doing a radio interview somewhere and she said if anybody's got any farm animals, bring 'em down.

TY ENGLAND: Stephanie apparently knew a farmer who had all kinds of farm animals. She made a deal with him to bring a herd of goats and sheep and I don't know what else to Garth's dressing room. You don't want to get pranked by Steph.

DAVE BUTZLER: They put all the little guys in the dressing room. They had this big ram in with them. Suddenly Garth comes through with a group of fan club people. I'm standing there because the little goats couldn't get up on the table, and I'm there feeding them bread. Wrong place, wrong time. That was when Garth—rightly, I should add!—came up with the saying, "A joke is a joke, but a prank will get you fired." We're like, "Well, how are we supposed to know the difference?" He goes, "I'll let you know." *(laughs)*

TY ENGLAND: I became Dave's roommate at that point, and, you know, a big night with Dave was sitting on the bed in your underwear, smoking a cigar and drinking a box of wine.

G: We got out there on the road and, damn, we stayed out there. Who wants to come home from the adventure of a lifetime? When your dreams start coming true, that's not the time to run for cover. *(laughs)* I never call it "working," but whatever it was . . . we were doing a lot of it. And I don't care what you do, if you're a doctor or a plumber or the Pope, sometimes you lose the thread. It's human. Things move so fast in life that it hits you all of a sudden, you question what you're doing. It happened to me one night, right in the middle of things being really big for us. I just lost my connection with what I was doing. Fortunately, I had the presence of mind to call the right person, and that was Allen Reynolds. I called him up in the middle of the tour, and I said, "I don't know what it is, but I can't get fired up, I can't . . . the fire isn't burning in my belly. I'm tired and I've got

THINGS MOVE SO FAST IN LIFE THAT IT HITS YOU ALL OF A SUDDEN,
you question what you're doing. - g

two more weeks' worth of shows before we get back to the States." I told him that the crowds were phenomenal, that everybody was treating us like kings, but I just couldn't get the fire. I'd never felt this feeling before. And he didn't do the usual thing. He didn't say, "Well, come on Garth, you guys are working really hard and should be exhausted." He didn't do what everybody else did. He just said, "Are you listening to what you're singing?" I remember sitting on the phone thinking, *What are you . . . it can't be that simple, can it?* Are you listening to what you're singing? Are you listening to the words that you either heard for the first time or wrote down for the first time that made you fall in love with them in the first place? And I'll be damned. It was one of those things where you're just trying to figure out what it is, and then Allen Reynolds said something so simple but right at the heart of what we do as live performers. The next night was Winnipeg, and, man, it was back. It might even have been better than it had ever been.

"WE WERE UP TO ABSOLUTELY NO GOOD.

We would sometimes be going out of our minds.
We had no satellite TV on the bus, no DVDs.
Just a deck of cards and an impulse to find new
ways to torture each other."
- TY ENGLAND

From the time of Garth Brooks' debut through *Ropin' the Wind*, there was no stopping.

The growth was exponential. As with any career of this kind, it was a matter of trying to keep your feet on the ground. When it happened to the Beatles, they had each other. George Harrison famously remarked that he didn't know how Elvis Presley handled his massive success as a solo artist. In the case of Garth Brooks, he created a middle position. Amidst the thrill and madness of the unrelenting early roadwork and its demands, he found ways for his band to bond as a band. They rented ice rinks and played hockey. Had shopping sprees and team dinners. They even went skiing, much to some of the band members' regret—though nothing was broken. But what it all meant was that the work, if only occasionally, was put to the side as the busiest band in popular music got a chance to see one another clearly, as humans having one of the wildest rides in entertainment history, but humans nonetheless.

7

THE TELEVISION SPECIALS!

SEPTEMBER 1991 | JUNE 1993

Television changed American life.

As the nation went through the dramatic changes of the 1950s and 1960s, the number of households with a television set went from under 1 million to 44 million. It would be hard to quantify the effects of this, whether in domestic life or at the level of human psychology.

But in popular music, it was clear that television was where the biggest careers would be forged. Elvis Presley, the Beatles, Frank Sinatra, Michael Jackson: All were catapulted to the upper reaches of their lives as entertainers when they connected with television audiences. The Beatles' 1964 performance on *The Ed Sullivan Show* demonstrated the remarkable impact of the still relatively new medium. But Presley's 1968 network comeback revealed the even greater power of a dedicated "special," focused solely on one artist.

In 1991, Garth Brooks was approached by NBC to do his first network special. No country artist had been offered that kind of spotlight before, and the effects would be lasting, not just for Garth but for country music as a whole. Viewership was massive. If the Garth Brooks phenomenon was already underway, the first NBC special was the rocket fuel that helped lift that phenomenon higher still. This was history in the making.

Some people are never going to buy a ticket, maybe because they can't afford it, maybe because of where they live . . . but, man, you still want them to see the show, to be a part of it.

TELEVISION MADE THAT POSSIBLE. -g

G: When we were out there doing fairs, loving the opening spots, still in some clubs but watching the music getting out there like never before, you could feel it building underneath the surface, like someone was pulling back a freaking slingshot. We were doing it just like Bob Doyle said we should: one by one by one. This fan base started to get energized and, I shit you not, when we were just ready to explode, NBC takes a chance on the first country artist doing a network special. "The Dance" and "Friends in Low Places" come out like a one-two punch. From there . . . I can't even define the next three years of our lives. I don't even remember a lot of it, it was moving so fast.

BOB DOYLE: As a network special, we were in front of a lot of eyeballs, but we didn't expect the ratings that came out of it. It all came together at this moment and gave us a platform to let the world see Garth Brooks on a much broader level.

TRISHA YEARWOOD: Unless you could really see Garth live, you didn't fully understand it. So the TV specials got a lot of people closer to the experience. I think it was huge for him. People who couldn't go see him live got to see a show, and a lot of them made up their minds that if they ever got a chance to see him live, they were going to do it.

it all came together at this
moment and gave us a platform to

LET THE WORLD SEE GARTH BROOKS ON A MUCH BROADER LEVEL."

— BOB DOYLE

G: Most of America knows Garth Brooks from the television specials, because, you know, 28 million people saw the first one in January of 1992. Well, we haven't sold 28 million tickets in our entire career. So in one hour, well . . . you see? I still can't completely believe it.

JOHN KINSCH: Well, honestly, the way I was looking at it was just another batch of shows. We were in the midst of getting the gear together because, slowly and steadily, everything was growing. For the Reunion Arena show, I knew it was being filmed and was a big deal. But I didn't really realize until I saw it on TV, then it kind of dawned on me . . . this isn't just a round of shows, this was a change in country music.

G: At the time, I don't know what this is going to mean for me. I don't think I'm smart enough to have any clue other than this: We're getting to play Texas, they're going to film it . . . so how do I make this look, when I close my eyes, like I'm standing up in the thirteenth row, I'm seventeen years old, and Freddie Mercury is onstage. How do I make it look that way?

JON SMALL: Garth grew up watching Kiss and guys like Billy Joel, watching artists that know how to entertain and feel that it's important to move around that stage. That was one of the things that I didn't understand for years, even after I shot many concerts with him.

TRISHA YEARWOOD: With a Garth show, there's tension, there's drama, there's anticipation. It's all very theatrical. You cannot discount Freddie Mercury and you cannot discount Kiss. You can't forget the theater of all of that, which really hooked him when he was young. That's part of this guy who comes out in his cowboy hat and his guitar. He wants to give people a show. I think you see James Taylor and Dan Fogelberg sitting in the same room with Gene Simmons and Freddie Mercury and . . . it works. The singer-songwriter with the acoustic guitar can also be the guy swinging from the rafters. It's a unique gift. It's who he is.

G: First and foremost, it was about the light rig. I'm crazy, I should be thinking about music, but I'm thinking about the light rig. Give it to me! So I get with Bandit and the guys, and they design a light rig that doesn't leave any space in the ceiling, none. This thing is so big it overlaps the stage, probably ten feet on all sides. It's got thousands of cans in it, all moving lights, all on individual motors. This thing is a beast. It throws unbelievable light. And they're lighting the audience, as well. You want to see the depth and you want to see the people, so we put the set list together, put the stage together, and put the light rig. We've got it all. The film company is coming in, and they're not ready for what they are going to be asked. And hats off to them for not having an ego that is so fucking big that they just ignored the artist! I told them, look, however many cameras you've got, take half of them and just comb the audience. Take them off us and put them on the people . . . and get ready to see what happens. These people that come to our shows are passionate as hell. It's like a freaking football game. They're going to come in their G gear and try to outsing you. I want to get that on camera.

DAVE BUTZLER: On some level, it was just another show. We were working, and there would be another show after this one, and another after that. We wanted them all to be great. But it was TV, and we were kind of new to it. We came to realize that this was going to be one of those things that people stopped what they were doing to watch, a kind of Super Bowl thing. But Garth wanted it to be our show. So Garth didn't just send us home that week and let the television people handle it. Welcome to Garth world, that's all I could really say. You gotta be in the moment.

MIKE PALMER: It was our first big television special, and we didn't really know what was going to happen. Garth always had some great ideas, most of them things I didn't know about until they were happening.

I'm standing in the thirteenth row, I'm seventeen years old, and
FREDDIE MERCURY IS ONSTAGE.
How do I make it look that way? -g

TRISHA YEARWOOD: I think even when the cameras aren't there, he's ready for them. He's a visual thinker, seeing how it all looks from the audience perspective. That's a big thing. The challenge is to give the viewer at home a sense of just how big it all is. You need those big crane shots, those boom shots where you see the whole crowd with their lighters lit.

DAN HEINS: It was a kind of multilevel set, meant to fit on big fair stages, that we expanded for the television special. It was Dave Gant and Mike Palmer on the sides. Mike wasn't in the center because that's where these bomb bay doors opened up, and that's where Garth entered. So the show would start, and these doors would open up and light would come out of them, into this smoke, and Garth would appear coming up this ramp, standing at the top of this thing with his arms up. It's a great moment that gets the crowd crazy. Some nights there was so much smoke on the stage you couldn't see the band. *(laughs)*

G: All the sudden we're in the TV land. So as an entertainer you're trying to think, *What is going to be the stamp, that defining moment that captures the energy of the show?* We knew we had a great show to deliver, but what was that one, new special moment? Like in movies, say *Terminator,* you know that shot where they totally destroy the whole building, just blow it up? Or in *The Dark Knight,* when the Joker stands up, dressed as a nurse, and blows up the entire hospital. There are peaks. We're thinking, *What's ours going to be?*

TY ENGLAND: There was a lot of thought given to how do you make an impact? Garth had a lot of conversations backstage, "Guys, what can we do?" What can we do that's significantly different that will embed this show in these people's minds? We always wanted to put on a good show, always wanted to impress our crowd. Garth would have a little brainstorm session about what we can do different. At one point,

> # HE'S A VISUAL THINKER,
> ## seeing how it all looks from the audience perspective.
> # THAT'S A BIG THING.
> ### - TRISHA YEARWOOD

James Garver—he's from Kansas, and said this in a very countrified way—just blurted out, "Smash guitars."

G: So at the "Friends in Low Places" moment, me and Ty, my college roommate, are going to line up across from each other, we're going to take our guitars, and we're going to do The Who, except this time . . . we're going to do it with two guitars against each, not beating a guitar against a floor. And, man, we had our moment.

TY ENGLAND: So it was decided that at the end of "Friends in Low Places," Garth and I would line up like we were standing in batter boxes and we'd bash our guitars against each other's. Garth called Takamine, the guitar makers, and told them what our plans were. We were shooting four nights, so they were kind enough to send us eight guitars. The problem was, they sent eight random guitars. None of them looked like Garth's main guitar, and none of them looked like my main guitar. I played a black Takamine that

I got in trade for the guitar my dad bought me in junior high school. It was kind of special to me. Garth sent people out all over Dallas and they found four guitars just like his, but they could only find three guitars like mine. So each night we'd have the big buildup through "Friends in Low Places," then we'd stand there and smash our guitars.

DAN HEINS: It was the fantastic moment in the room. The energy was amazing. It was right at the end of "Friends in Low Places," when the band was getting ready to hit that last note. Mark Greenwood had removed all the internal bracing of the guitars, so man, when they hit, those things just splintered, went everywhere. It was like an explosion onstage, right at the downbeat. With the lights and the crowd . . . it was electric.

TY ENGLAND: Because they'd taken most of the bracing out of Garth's guitar, it would almost powder on impact. So this went on, first night, second night, third night. On the fourth night, Garth and I were backstage, and I think he had this feeling that my guitar had a special meaning to me. It was the same one he'd borrowed for the "Tomorrow Never Comes" video. He'd used it on all of his stills. That guitar covered a lot of ground. So he comes up to me and says, "Pal, if you don't want to, we don't have to smash tonight. I get it." I thought that was pretty cool, you know. But I looked at this poor guitar, saw where my belt buckle had almost worn through the back of it. I thought, *You know, I can't think of a better way to memorialize this guitar than to smash it onstage tonight.* And we did it. At the end of the night, I gathered all the black parts of my guitar I could find, stuffed them in the case, and on we went. That guitar ended up being in the Country Music Hall of Fame.

BOB DOYLE: I remember one day during the tapings, there with Garth in the dressing room. We were just sitting with the lights turned off. Kind of a quiet moment, reflecting. Here we were, playing an arena, doing a network television special that was going to be broadcast coast to coast. It was one of these milestones. We kind of looked back on the goals and aspirations we'd had just a few years before. And here we are. It's being actualized. But, you know, Garth had a vision. He was going to incorporate what he did live within the stage set that he'd imagined and designed, and he was going to work with the director to get it right. Step by step, he was executing on something that he'd seen in his head. He's a very visual person. Looking at the stage and watching that show, I could see these elements he'd talked about over the previous months. They'd probably been in his mind for years. And there they were.

G: After that, it seemed like every time you turned around we were on TV, video channels, magazines, all over. We felt what a major network special could do. We were running so fast that you just couldn't, you couldn't take a breath. And the truth is, you didn't want one.

"With the lights and crowd . . .

IT WAS
ELECTRIC."
— DAN HEINS

"These people that come to our shows are **PASSIONATE AS HELL.** It's like a freaking football game."

-g

This Is Garth Brooks would be seen by over 28 million Americans. In the same month as the Reunion Arena shows that would become the centerpiece of that television special, a third Garth Brooks album hit the shelves. It would become a thing of legend. It was called *Ropin' the Wind*. Of course, it wasn't as if *No Fences* was over. In fact, it wasn't like Garth Brooks' debut was over. Both releases were alive and well on the radio, on the charts, and in the hearts of fans. But *Ropin'* was dropped right into the middle of all that momentum, becoming the first album by a country artist ever to debut at number one not just on Billboard's country charts but on the industry pop charts. *Ropin'* bumped Metallica . . . and made a comfortable spot for itself right there at the top of it all. By the time *This Is Garth Brooks* aired in January 1992, there was a country music revolution underway, and more often than not it went by the name Garth Brooks. No more was country music the quiet cousin in

American entertainment. Everything had changed. Country music was defining the era.

Behind the scenes, something else happened in 1991 that made the Garth Brooks phenomenon more striking still: the introduction of a thing called SoundScan. Where for years the calculations of album sales had come about through calls to distracted record store clerks who all but guessed at the numbers of records they'd sold any given week, suddenly the marketplace had a tracking system. And country records were moving like nothing else, with Garth Brooks leading the sales. It was a testament to who was out there. For the first time, the audience for country music could not be denied.

THE WORD ON THE STREETS WAS THAT YOU *HAD* TO SEE HIM LIVE. IF HIS SUCCESS ELEVATED COUNTRY MUSIC AS A WHOLE, HE WAS IN A CLASS BY HIMSELF.

But how does an artist take what is already an unprecedented success . . . even higher? The world was about to see. With the second NBC special,

This Is Garth Brooks, Too!, Brooks would show himself to be the kind of entertainer who comes along only once a generation. And it would happen on the stage. As the diehard fans already knew, the songs that broke Garth Brooks on radio were almost overshadowed by the way the artist made that material come alive in performance. The word on the streets was that you *had* to see him live. If his success elevated country music as a whole, he was in a class by himself when it came to performance, and the Texas Stadium shows took the whole experience to the next level. What Garth Brooks was doing up there on the stage was a brand-new thing for country. There would be fire and there would be rain. Images of Brooks flying above the crowd would become iconic. Shooting those three shows at Texas Stadium in 1993 allowed Brooks to show another massive television audience that the story hadn't ended at *Ropin' the Wind*. Quite the opposite. The congregation was growing, as was the spectacle. The Garth Brooks show was at a new peak, breaking records in ticket and album sales . . . and showing no signs of slowing down.

"TO ME, TEXAS STADIUM WAS MONUMENTAL."

- JON SMALL

It needed to
REACH OUT AND GRAB THAT AUDIENCE. -g

BOB DOYLE: By the time we do the second NBC special, everything had gotten bigger for Garth. The special itself would follow suit. What struck me was the scale of it, the incorporation of the entire stadium within the production he came up with, the flying, the rain and the fire. It was a massive endeavor. It was a matter of executing on some bold ideas, giving Garth the opportunity to really use his imagination, and it looked great on television.

STEVE COX: Sometimes he'll be trying to tell us, "We need to get it there." And we'll be like, "Huh? Where? What are you talking about?" And then, when we finally do get it there, it's like, "Oh, we understand now!" We're all experienced players, but he's just got this vision of what he wants to get to.

JON SMALL: To me, Texas Stadium was monumental. First of all, what I saw was all the money they spent to make this look so good. Nobody wants to spend money, and the networks never spend money, so I knew it had to be coming from Garth. When I was growing up, my mother always said to me, "Invest in yourself." That's what Garth did. He just invested in himself and in his audience, putting the money into this monumental show that could translate on television.

G: The intervening years, the ones between the two NBC specials, are the blink of an eye. *Ropin' the Wind* would become the son of *No Fences,* which I never thought would happen because *Fences* was so huge. But *Ropin'* got itself right in there. It just became the beast, and it was crazy because it didn't have "Friends in Low Places," it didn't have "Thunder Rolls," yet it kept *No Fences* out of the number one slot its entire life. On the pop charts, I think you're looking at number 1, 3, and 13. On the country charts, you're looking at number 1, 2, and 3. And it would go a whole year like that. Off *Ropin'* there would be "Rodeo," "Shameless," "What She's Doin' Now," and, I think, "Papa Loved Mama" and "The River." It delivered five singles. *Ropin'* was the first and only record that did that for us. Radio was going through them quick. The second NBC special, this time at Texas Stadium, was coming with that kind of wind at its back. It needed to reach out and grab that audience.

"Standing Outside the Fire"? WE'RE GOING TO FILL THE WHOLE STAGE WITH FLAMES. BIG FLAMES. -g

JON SMALL: They didn't use video screens at the time of the Texas Stadium show. So everybody was looking at this one-inch-tall guy onstage, which meant he had to work ten times as hard to reach everybody, and that's why he would run around a lot, going from the back of the stage to the front of the stage to engage that audience. And, look, it's a very hard thing. I've seen so many artists in these gigantic arenas or stadiums that just can't reach the audience unless they have video.

G: You're looking at Texas Stadium as opposed to Reunion Arena, not that far from each other, still Dallas/Fort Worth area. But the difference is simple: This time you're going to do a huge-ass stadium show. Everything has to be bigger. All the way down to, the shirt you're wearing has to be brighter. But now with "Standing Outside the Fire," we're going to fill the whole stage with flames. Big flames. "Thunder Rolls"? This time it's going to rain inside the stadium. And then, in an effort to make those people who fill those back seats know you care about their experience, you're going to fly across the stadium and end up right in their face. This was all on the sketch pad. So here come the engineers.

JOHN MCBRIDE: I mean he found a way to go through the air and get to those seats at the back. He loved flying through the air. He loved doing things that make your jaw drop. I mean we carried massive lighting rigs and big sound, and, you know, he just loved putting it all on the stage.

201

JIMMY MATTINGLY: Garth has this ability to make everybody that's in there think he's looking right at them, singing right to them. He picks people out in the back of the venue and says, "I've got to reach the guy back there in that blue shirt." And to that guy, that's unbelievable. He'll never forget that experience. I think the thing that makes Garth different than a lot of people is that he knows that each one of those people went way out of their way to come see that show. He doesn't feel like he's doing them some big favor by being there. I think he feels the other way, that they're doing him a favor by being there.

MIKE PALMER: I remember walking in, walking down the tunnel, and seeing this massive line of pipe and this other water line. I didn't even realize what this was for. I didn't know it was for the gas for the fire for "Standing Outside the Fire" and the water for "The Thunder Rolls." So it was huge. You try not to let it eat at your nerves, but . . .

DAVE BUTZLER: We thought the engineering and staging was done right, you know, because engineers had signed off on everything. But there were certain things we learned after, like that they needed to load weight in particular areas to counter the weight in the middle. But none of that was brought to us on production load-in day.

He loved doing things that
MAKE YOUR JAW DROP.
- JOHN MCBRIDE

G: Anybody who's watched the Cowboys a lot on TV will notice that from 1994 on there's a set of what they call "the Garth bars." They connect to three holes in the top of Texas Stadium. We hung the production off those. On one of the days leading up, I was offsite at CEMA distribution, and I'm with radio reps. The phone rings, and it's Kelly at that stadium. He says, "Garth, you're going to need to get back to the stadium now." I ask him what's happening. "Just get here now," he tells me. By the time I'm arriving back at the stadium, there's helicopters everywhere. In the car, on CNN all you hear is "Garth Brooks . . . Texas . . ." And I think, *Oh, shit.*

JOHN KINSCH: They hung the superstructure, and it was supposed to hold all of our stuff. Three hours into hanging everything on the rig, it broke. I've heard the story told a half a dozen different ways, but I just know I was standing under it when it broke.

G: It's hanging down in a V but it's not on the stage, just hanging over it. It snapped in half, but it's still connected, which probably made all the difference. The worst that came of it, thank God, was a broken ankle. But now we've got this thing hanging over

"I was standing under it
WHEN IT BROKE."
– JOHN KINSCH

the stage. We're immediately doing production meetings, and you can barely hear each other over the helicopters. We're screaming over them, trying to figure out what the hell we're going to do. The first thing is everyone's safety. Once we are sure everyone is okay, it comes down to a decision of whether we cancel the show or not. And we decided to move forward.

He picks people out in the back of the venue and says,

"I'VE GOT TO REACH THE GUY BACK THERE IN THAT BLUE SHIRT." AND TO THAT GUY, THAT'S UNBELIEVABLE.

- JIMMY MATTINGLY

G: The first night was just a nightmare. It felt like nothing went right. So after that, I'm trying to figure it out—it's a stadium, not an arena, so what can we do here?—and I'm thinking about all the things we can do different the next two nights. I walk into the hotel room, look in the hotel room bathroom, and there's a pregnancy test that's positive. We're having a second child. This is all after this first night. *(laughs)* I lay down in the bed, and I'm thinking, *Holy cow, we have another kid coming* and, *Holy cow, on "We Shall Be Free" we need the choir to come in earlier down the ramps. (laughs)* I'm thinking about all these things, and they're having karaoke downstairs in the atrium. It's loud, and I'm laying there with all this stuff in my head, but I'm never one of those guys that calls over down to the front desk to complain about the noise. And then they start singing "Friends in Low Places."

MIKE PALMER: They took Garth up and flew him all the way across the stadium during, I think, "Ain't Goin' Down ('Til the Sun Comes Up)." In the end, it all worked. He flew every night.

"IT WAS AN UNBELIEVABLE THREE DAYS OF MUSIC

in that stadium." - g

VICKI HAMPTON: He would never give himself that kind of credit, but he killed it. That show was rock and roll. He's just all about the awe and the wow factor. His imagination goes far and wide. But the magic for me was when we were walking out on that stage, not hearing myself speak because the screams from the audience were so loud. That gave me goosebumps. That made me realize the magnitude and the impact he had on people. For "We Shall Be Free" there was a massive choir, all lined up in robes, appearing as if they came out of nowhere. All the details were there.

TY ENGLAND: It wasn't just lights, it was having rain and fire inside a stadium. Just beyond anything you've seen up to that point.

G: In the end, everything went great. The rain didn't work the first night, didn't work the second night, but on the third night it worked like a charm. Beautiful. It was good. The fire worked great all three nights. And I got to fly all three nights. I was so close to the crowd, I felt somebody touch my boot. It was awesome. Those people's faces were fabulous. It was an unbelievable three days of music in that stadium, and the end result was gorgeous, bigger than life, exactly what we needed at that point of the trip.

I WAS SO CLOSE TO THE CROWD,
I felt somebody touch my boot.
It was awesome.
- g

The success of the NBC specials established a new precedent in country music.

Garth Brooks brought the boom times. The possibilities were more vast than ever for *all* country music artists because they were shown that the big career was possible. A kind of success that hadn't existed before Brooks came along was now a part of country's history. But the television specials also demonstrated the degree to which the Garth Brooks live show was at the heart of his success. He'd always had the songs, the team, the connection with fans . . . but the performances that he delivered night after night put all of that together. It came through in the first NBC special . . . but the second NBC special drove the point home in ways no one expected. Brooks found a new high, and brought his fans along with him.

Both overseas and at home, more and more people came out to the shows because they'd seen Garth Brooks on television. You could say it was further proof that the audience, always discerning, knew what was real and what was good. They could tell when it was honest, when it was about the truth, about the joy. But you also had to marvel at the way in which the magic that had launched Garth Brooks in the clubs was the same magic that carried him across the world, whether in arenas, stadiums, or on television screens. The biggest marker of his success was that he brought the intimacy and sincerity of his shows wherever he went. And it meant that more people than ever before knew just where country music could get them: in the heart.

8

OVER THERE!

MAY 16, 1997

Popular music has a long history of crisscrossing the Atlantic.

Perhaps most famously, the British Invasion of the sixties brought the Beatles, the Rolling Stones, the Animals, the Kinks, and so many more rock and roll bands across the water and straight to the top of the American charts. Music, the universal language, connected the two shores. It was a cross-fertilization that would change popular culture and force audiences in the United States to consider their own nation's musical legacy from another angle, as it was reproduced and honored by these young, mostly British acts.

Paradoxically, at the heart of the British Invasion was . . . American music, in particular, the blues tradition that had emerged out of the American South. But what of country music? How had country impacted European audiences?

The truth was, sounds of Nashville had only intermittently found a place on European soil. Those same British acts that had made an investment in the American blues made occasional circuits through country music's vast library of song. Keith Richards of the Rolling Stones, to name one example, was known to play songs associated with Tammy Wynette, George Jones, and Merle Haggard. But compared to the blues, country music didn't get its rightful attention. Only in the case of Johnny Cash had a country act begun to really crack the European market. But that was all about to change, and the tour that brought Garth Brooks and his band across the waters played a key role. In the end, it was the invasion in reverse. Brooks brought a classic country sound, with deep roots in the music of the British Isles. When audiences heard the sound, they found something of themselves in there. This guy, after all, was part of the family. And that's how he was welcomed.

Sometimes you have to

LEAVE HOME

to find out just who you are. -g

G: It was really moving to find that people who weren't raised like you could connect with your traditions. Cowboys and rodeos, that kind of stuff is so American you'd think it just won't always mean the same thing outside of our own country. But I think it's worked because we've gone after the songs that have a message inside them, songs that may be dressed in the Western motif but that you can get even if you didn't grow up in the States. Like there's some human truth inside the stories that has room for everyone. Maybe that's why the stuff was resonating with people outside the U.S.

JOHN KINSCH: The crowds were crazy. There was one general admission show where Garth changed guitars, and somehow one of them got pulled into the audience, and it was shredded. I'm like, *Holy shit . . . maybe we should step back from the edge of the stage about six feet.*

G: A blessing is that every day you get to go out and learn. We were never in a place where we weren't learning something new. Cities like Munich, Dublin, Barcelona, Glasgow, unbelievable. Sheffield and Birmingham in England were just like playing for Kansas or Oklahoma. Like, these were the hardworking people you were raised with, you know?

DAVE GANT: We went from Ireland to England to Switzerland and then back to Germany. It was my first time out of the country. Everybody's first time out the country, I think.

"EVERYBODY KNEW THE WORDS TO THE SONGS, COULD SING THEM LIKE THEY WERE POETRY."

- BOB DOYLE

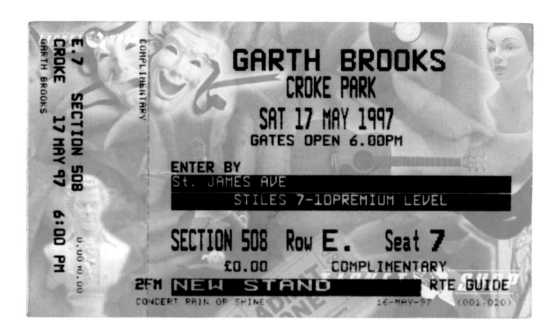

Ticket: GARTH BROOKS / CROKE PARK / SAT 17 MAY 1997 / GATES OPEN 6.00PM / ENTER BY St. JAMES AVE / STILES 7-10PREMIUM LEVEL / SECTION 508 Row E. Seat 7 / £0.00 COMPLIMENTARY / 2FM NEW STAND RTE GUIDE / CONCERT RAIN OR SHINE 16-MAY-97 (001.020)

MARK GREENWOOD: Europe was really interesting because every country was so different. Travel for three hours and the culture changes. You go to Austria, and they're very reserved but very attentive. The Germans can be a little bit more raucous.

G: We were at this one dinner, all of us, and it's like a ten-course meal. Just happens there's ten of us. So we decided that each person had to be the first person to try a course. Some of the things coming out were pretty damn new to us. *(laughs)* So you take your turn. I see mine coming out, and I'm thinking I got lucky because I got spaghetti, something I recognized. But I'm starting to eat it, and something is not right about this spaghetti, it's just different. That's when I hear from somewhere back in the kitchen that I got the baby eels. That was a little tough. But, again, the people were so sweet, nobody trying to pull anything over you. We were learning about their traditional way to eat over there.

DAVE GANT: I think we were over there a month or six weeks. Then we came home, had summer months off, and then we went over to Australia for three weeks, then back to Europe.

G: The first thing they tell you when you're going to head over is to leave your pedal steel and fiddle at home. This is what the industry tells you. But I'm thinking, *That makes no sense.* Why in the world would you change the music that you're selling, make it different from what's on the records? They don't remix the albums, so there are steel and fiddles on those same recordings that European audiences are buying. But you should avoid being what? Too country? That's what they seemed to be suggesting by telling us not to have those things onstage. I said, "Forget that, we're going to go over there, and we're going to play with twin fiddles and pedal steel because that's what we do. And if it sticks, we'll be back, and if it doesn't stick, I'm not going to bother you with it again but thanks for the opportunity to get to play." So the first time over there was a little rough, and it was one of those things that you just kind of did. You went over there and played London and a few other places. But, in '94, we took the full freak show with us. We took it all: stage, lighting, everything. We document it all, get it on film. We start at The Point in Dublin, Ireland, and I can't remember how many shows we did there, but it was a ton, and Ireland just took us in. It was like, holy cow. I'm worried these people might think I'm somebody else! I just don't get this. They were fabulous. Just the best, and it gave us the confidence to move on into Europe.

BOB DOYLE: I think the thing that surprised us was this lyrical sensibility in Ireland. Everybody knew the words to the songs, could sing them like they were poetry.

G: It was crazy in Dublin. There's a promoter there named Jim Aiken, and he said, "Look, I'm going to put you at The Point, but I'm telling you it won't hold you." I thought this was Dublin's biggest indoor venue, a large room, so I said, "What do you mean it won't hold us, isn't it a big place?" He said, "Well, yes, it's 8,500 capacity, but it just won't hold you. You'll have to do . . . maybe six shows." I'm thinking, *Are you serious?* He nods. I thought, *Oh, he's just a promoter.* But I'll be damned, they sold out like nine shows, and each one of them was freaking awesome. It was like leaving home to go to the Super Bowl. Those beautiful people in the audience knew every word. Every word. They were singing in Ireland before they sang in the States. We'd never seen anything like it.

> The first thing they tell you when you're going to head over is to leave your pedal steel and fiddle at home. This is what the industry tells you. But I'm thinking,
> # THAT MAKES NO SENSE. -g

DAVE BUTZLER: It's another thing altogether being in an arena and having all those people singing that loud and clear. That's what got me. They were into it, man, heart and soul.

DAVE GANT: It was nuts, there were people waiting at the airport. The first NBC special had aired in Ireland, too. The Irish picked up on that. I could walk down the street in Dublin and have someone go, "Dave?" People would recognize band members. Supposedly one in four Irish have got a Garth CD. It's one of these big deals. All sorts of people came to The Point, the U2 guys were showing up. It was pretty wild. It caught us off guard the first time around.

TY ENGLAND: The Point blew us all away. Because we were used to crowds being passionate, because at that point we were playing for crowds that were louder than we could become. But this was overwhelming. It just filled you with this energy that fed us. That the crowd sang the entire show to us. Word for word. They would literally take the songs over and sing them back to us.

BOB DOYLE: I know Garth was moved to tears. It was like, wait, how do they know this music so well? I think we did nine shows. And who knows how many we could have done. It was quite an experience.

G: Then we roll into Germany. And Germany was phenomenal, too. But when we get to Berlin, where they have the Deutschlandhalle, the Fest Hall, this is where it started to get real for me. Something happened that really affected me. This place we're playing was built by Hitler for the '36 Olympics and after that was where he gave his public speeches. When you're in this place, believe me, it's haunted, just knowing that massive Nazi rallies were held in this place you're about to perform. Then, it's a capacity crowd, and you start to sing "We Shall Be Free," and that audience sings it back to you. In that moment, something happens for me. It hits me like a ton of bricks. You just can't help but see the power of music, its ability to bring people together. On some level, I can't believe I had to go all the way here to figure this out, but in that moment, in that place, it's no longer about getting your food free backstage or riding a bus across the world with your buddies. This is about making the world you're in a better place while you're here. Probably every artist comes to that epiphany. This was mine. And I felt proud to be there, singing, a small part of something much bigger, something good, something powerful. Bringing music around the world, as much as it was a privilege, also became more of a mission. This room we were in wasn't built because of love, but that night love was filling the seats.

MIKE PALMER: Depending on the night, you didn't necessarily know what you needed to be ready for. There was a kind of adventure to it that was different from the States.

G: One thing we learned on the first trip over was that we wouldn't do interviews unless whoever was interviewing us had seen the show. The rule was, you get the interview once you've seen that show but not before. And I got to tell you, one hundred times out of a hundred, if they saw the show, they got it, and the interview went just fine. And one hundred times out of one hundred, when we didn't stick to that rule, they could be the most embarrassing times of your life, because they would start the interview by asking, "So do you ride a horse onstage?" Or, "Is there smoke coming out of the bottom of your jeans?" *(laughs)* You're like, what the hell?

BOB DOYLE: Not everyone in the press was ready to embrace this new artist doing this very American music.

G: Wherever you go, even in the States, there are people who think country music is *Hee Haw*. But people that know country music know that *Hee Haw* is just entertainment, it's country music people poking fun at themselves but nothing like the truth of country music. On the other hand, the people that don't know country music, they might just think that's what country music is. When we went over to Europe, the people in the audience understood. They were phenomenal. The people in the press often understood, particularly if they'd seen the show. Some said, "Okay, I've seen the show, and it totally changed my mind." But then there were the ones that, well, you were marked the second you came on their show. Country music was truly foreign to them. They'd treat you very differently from when they're interviewing, let's say, Aerosmith. Aerosmith is clearly influenced by the Beatles and Rolling Stones. So they're going to have a lot to talk about, and there's not going to be much need for explaining. It's rock and roll, and they're familiar with rock and roll. But they weren't familiar with country music. George Jones? Merle Haggard? Sometimes they had a cartoon in their heads—so we had to work against that. That's why we needed them to come out and see the show. Then they could make their own judgment. The audiences, well, they already had.

"In that moment, in that place, it's no longer about getting your food free backstage or riding a bus across the world with your buddies.

THIS IS ABOUT MAKING THE WORLD YOU'RE IN A BETTER PLACE WHILE YOU'RE HERE."

- g

JOHN KINSCH: We did a show in Spain, Barcelona, I think. It was an Olympic basketball arena, 18,000 seats or something. We heard they'd only sold 6,000 seats. By the end of that day it was sold out. That was all walk-ups. The people were ready for this, you know?

G: We went into places like Sweden and Scotland, met all these very sweet people, Switzerland, and then, we headed back home. I got to hug Taylor, my baby, who was sicker than a dog, and got to be around her while she got better, got up and running around. Then here comes August, our second daughter . . . life just kept going, bringing abundance at a very rapid pace. It seemed like in a blink of an eye, we were heading off to Australia.

THESE PEOPLE WERE JUST GOING TO ENGULF HIM.

- TRACY GREENWOOD

BOB DOYLE: They had part of the summer off, then went to Australia. Garth came in wanting to work, and he really got it.

G: August isn't ten days old yet when we get on a plane for Australia. You should have seen the passengers when Sandy and I walked on with a newborn baby and a two-year-old child for an eighteen-hour flight. People were just, *ohhh.* I couldn't blame them. But those two babies were phenomenal. Phenomenal. It was like, thank you, God. If the rest of the tour doesn't even go well, I'm okay. *(laughs)* After a few New Zealand shows, our first stop in Australia was Sydney. Damn, it's like playing Los Angeles, like playing the Forum! This place is rocking, and we're all looking at each other going, "This is going to be a great tour down here." We went everywhere from Brisbane over to Perth. I'll tell you, Brisbane, that's a place you want to play. There's a video we made for "Ain't Going Down ('Til the Sun Comes Up)" that we shot there and some other spots on the world tour. People in the U.S. just assume it's all done in the States. It sure looks like we're home! That's how good the audiences were. I'd say to people, "Wait a minute, you don't understand, that's Germany, that's Glasgow, this is Sydney, and so on." No one could believe it because these kids look like American country music fans. So we added each country's flag in the video so people would know it was from the world tour. Then they got it. That told a story. This is how the whole world around us is reacting to this. Close your eyes in Sydney, you were in the Forum. Close your eyes in Brisbane, you're at Rupp Arena in Kentucky. You fight your way in and fight your way out, and it's a blast the whole way. There's this one shot in the video where it all goes so stupidly crazy in Brisbane . . . I jump from the stage to this railing, over the railing into the crowd and just start heading up into the crowd . . . one of the most fun places ever. And people were traveling for days

"THE ENERGY OF CROKE PARK, THOSE 50,000 BEAUTIFUL PEOPLE,

was like nothing I'd ever felt."

- TRISHA YEARWOOD

to get there. Those people are passionate about their music. They see past where you're from. And they just lock in to what they love about the music. That whole tour changed the way we saw our place in the world. But it would be Croke Park in Dublin . . . wow.

TRACY GREENWOOD: Croke Park was the return to Ireland, to Dublin, in 1997. Unlike Central Park, where I was worried if they were going to embrace him, in Ireland I'm thinking our crew better be ready, because these people were just going to engulf him. And they did. He loves the people of Ireland. They were perfect shows.

TRISHA YEARWOOD: Ireland is that way. They know their music, all kinds of music. They love country music, embrace you like family. With Garth, it's almost like he's this ambassador. I don't think there's a person in Ireland that doesn't know and love Garth Brooks. And the love is mutual. There is some kind of special relationship with Croke Park in particular. I was there to witness it.

G: We'd announced Central Park, which is coming in August of '97. Croke Park was in May that year. So we roll back into Ireland, and when we see this place in Dublin, holy cow. Half of it's under construction, but try to remember, you can fit three football fields, three NFL football fields, on a Gaelic football field. This thing was humongous. It was gorgeous. It was about 45,000 people, festival seating. Three shows. Festival seating means the audience is as close to the stage as they can get. And they want to get close!

I DON'T THINK THERE'S A PERSON IN IRELAND THAT DOESN'T KNOW AND LOVE GARTH.
- TRISHA YEARWOOD

G: Jon Small was shooting this. I think we did Thursday, Friday, Saturday. The first night, in the handshake before the show, we all have our hands in the middle, and I said, "Guys, you know this place, they love you, you love them, there can be nothing but great things happening here tonight, so let's go out and just get a stake in the ground and build on it the next couple nights, do whatever you need to do."

JON SMALL: I brought all the cameras I could from London, and everything else came from America. We had to barge everything over. You land in England, and then you have to put all your equipment on barges and get it to Ireland. It's quite heavy. We had the biggest film order ever, over 400,000 feet of film. Because we shot three nights there and each camera had four people. There's a cameraman, there's an assistant cameraman, and then there are two others, a third assistant and a fourth assistant—for each camera! You needed four on each because, basically, the camera only runs for eight minutes before it's out of film. So the crew is constantly at work. Garth must have some kind of record because there are hundreds and hundreds of cans of film. The crew was just gigantic.

> It doesn't matter how you start,
> # IT MATTERS HOW YOU FINISH.
> - MIKE PALMER

G: We go out there on our first night and it is, it's unbelievable. And I can't explain it, but I see this vision. There's a white film just all over the crowd. Like a real thin fog, and it's the most religious experience I've ever had in my life. You're playing to these people and . . . they're you, you're them. There is no separation. It's almost like you're breathing in at the same time they're breathing in, and it is . . . it is just spiritual.

TRISHA YEARWOOD: It was the first time that I'd sung onstage with Garth. Just by chance, I was in Ireland doing my own tour, and he invited me to come and be a part of Croke Park. So I sang backup with everybody else. I was a part of the band. It was really special for me. My memory of it is walking out and being overwhelmed. I may have sung in front of a Garth crowd before, but I had never been in front of a Garth crowd with Garth onstage. It was a whole different ballgame. I remember going off stage after I did my first few songs, being underneath the stage, and there was some kind of Irish whiskey there. Now I'm not a big drinker, but I was like, I'm having a shot of that before I go back up there. *(laughs)* I was terrified and deeply moved. The energy of Croke Park, those 50,000 beautiful people, was like nothing I'd ever felt.

G: For the first time ever, there's Trisha Yearwood, Trisha and Susan Ashton, doing the background vocals. So you're playing with your buddies, the people you love. There's Jim Mattingly, there's Palmer, and there's Trisha, and . . . everything just went perfect. After one night, Jon Small comes up to me and goes, "I've got everything I need." It's crazy. It was that good.

JOHN KINSCH: Croke Park was awesome. It rained every day up until the show. *(laughs)* Dublin was . . . it could have been Dallas. It could've been Cheyenne. Just the ferocity of the fandom.

MARK GREENWOOD: I'd gone from being on the crew to being in the band. And that was my first big onstage thing. Fifty thousand people? The show starts, and, without me expecting it, Garth throws me an intro solo. *(laughs)* I was like, "I'm still pretty new at this gig, you know?" I still felt like an impostor.

MIKE PALMER: That's just the way Garth believes in you and believes in what happens out there. He's always had a motto, a sports analogy, "Lose early win late." Like, it doesn't matter how you start, it matters how you finish. He doesn't mind flying by the seat of his pants. I think he prefers it. It's like, let's get in there and we'll figure out the intro when we're there. Croke was beautiful. And, of course, Garth is getting up there on the second story, it was actually higher than two stories, but up there in the scaffolding and doing crazy stuff.

G: When we go back for the encore that first night, to do "The River," I tell the guys that I'm going to do something I haven't before, something that will be like the guitar smashing, a kind of stamp. I let the audience pass me around, hand to hand, as I sing "The River." I told them, "Look, there are three things: I gotta keep my hat, because it's for the show, I gotta keep this mic so I can sing and be heard, and the third is . . . well, we all know what you don't touch, right?" *(laughs)* And here it began. It was so freaking cool.

TRISHA YEARWOOD: There was a kind of mosh pit, and he went right into it. The audience passed him around, hand to hand. He's on his back, and they're passing him around in this circle and . . . only in Ireland. Such trust and such mutual love.

G: The two things I remember most were, first, you just felt safe, you had a hundred hands on you but you just felt safe, and, second, was hearing in your ear each individual voice as you passed them. All these wonderful Irish voices. One by one in my ear. It's like the perfect amount of perfume on a woman where you don't smell it before you get to her, you don't smell it after you move past, but while you're there with her, it's like, oh, the scent!

DAVE BUTZLER: Kids were just passing him around. I think he touched every person in that stadium, far and near. I don't know why, there's just always been something about the Irish.

JON SMALL: Garth came up with the idea of having two helicopters fly over the stadium. One helicopter was on top of the other, one filming through the blades of the first to see the people below. It was a somewhat dangerous situation, but I found these amazing young pilots from the armed forces, and we painted the helicopters with G's on them. The first helicopter was only, say, 200 feet, 300 feet above the crowd, and then on top of that was the other, shooting down.

G: The big shot I wanted was the helicopter over the crowd and, above that, a shot of the first helicopter taken from a second one above it.

DAVE BUTZLER: The one helicopter was over that other helicopter, and that was scarier than shit. Garth's out there surfing the crowd, these two helicopters above him. Because of that shot and our director Jon Small, they now have a rule of no helicopters around the stadiums. *(laughs)*

G: We still use that shot every chance we get, to this day. It's beautiful. People talk about Central Park being the crown jewel of our touring history, and I understand why that is. But three months before Central Park was shot, Croke Park happened, and I'm as proud of that as anything we've done. Words just don't do it justice. But now we have two more nights to go. And I don't know how to say this, but it was fucking better Friday than it was Thursday! It's just one of those times that you just never want to end.

TRISHA YEARWOOD: In filming Croke Park, they also got behind-the-scenes. Everybody wants to see that, and more and more Garth's all about accessibility, showing people every aspect of his life, just to give even more of a sense of who he is, on and off stage. But Garth was going through a lot right around that time. In work and in life.

JIMMY MATTINGLY: I think at that time, Garth's mom was going through some health issues. He was getting some bad news from home about her. It was just one of those times where we needed what the audience was giving back. He needed it, you know? And it was just unbelievable. It had a magic to it.

G: I had my mom on my mind. And at the same time, there were things going on with work. Jim Fifield, the CEO of Capitol Records, was there at Croke Park. This was during a time when the label had for some reason kind of forgotten Nashville. They'd just kind of let Nashville run on autopilot. So Fifield finds me in Ireland because it's closer to London, where he's at, and in between the last show and the encore we sit down for a few minutes, while these people are still out there, waiting for the next song. And in those few minutes, we get from "Hi, how ya doin'," to "I ain't making another fucking record for your company until somebody comes to take a look at the Nashville label." Truth was, I knew they were getting ready to sell the label. But they always go, "We're not trying to sell." But they had totally left the farm, and nobody was coming to check on it. So the last thing I told him before I went to do "The River" was, "No, I'm not interested at all in making a record, not for this regime, because I just don't feel anybody is at home." And then I went back on the stage and enjoyed one of the greatest feelings ever in my life. But that's how this business happens, how life happens, the highs and the lows happen within seconds of each other. The highest of highs and lowest of lows.

BOB DOYLE: He went out there as if on a mission.

> ### I feel like I found a home over there, A HOME AS REAL AS ANY IN MY LIFE. -g

JIMMY MATTINGLY: They're very musical over there, singing every word. The people can bring it. Garth's voice, too, I think kind of lends itself to these things. Those ballads, like "The River." Oh my God. They came unglued.

VICKI HAMPTON: Croke Park was when I really got to see the magnitude of how Garth affects people, because they were fainting all over the place. Just collapsing. They've got people carrying folks out. It was just unbelievable to watch. He didn't have to sing, because they carried it all the way to the end.

G: Thursday was unreal and Friday was unbelievable—you don't want to push your luck, so I told the band, "Just go out there and give it your all, we've already won." And then, I'm telling you, Saturday was the best night. These three nights . . . it was just eerie, really spiritual for me. I feel like I found a home over there. A home as real as any in my life.

"The two things I remember most were, first, you just felt safe, you had a hundred hands on you but you just felt safe, and, second, was hearing in your ear each individual voice as you passed them. All these wonderful Irish voices."

-g

"Kids were just passing him around. I think he touched every person in that stadium, far and near. I don't know why, there's just always been something about the Irish."

- DAVE BUTZLER

After the Garth Brooks World Tour that included musical homecomings in Ireland, England, Australia, Spain, Germany, and more, country music became a fixture in Europe and beyond. At festivals, in clubs, in foreign languages, country music had found another home. Country music sales and tours took off outside North America for the first time ever. Not only did the world awaken to the fresh sounds of country music, but back in America, country fans were starting to realize that their beloved traditions were at last finding a global audience. And what that meant was that maybe, just maybe, everybody on the planet had a lot more in common than we thought. For the artists, that meant more opportunities and more fans. Country music had undergone another crucial crossover . . . this time over an ocean and across a globe.

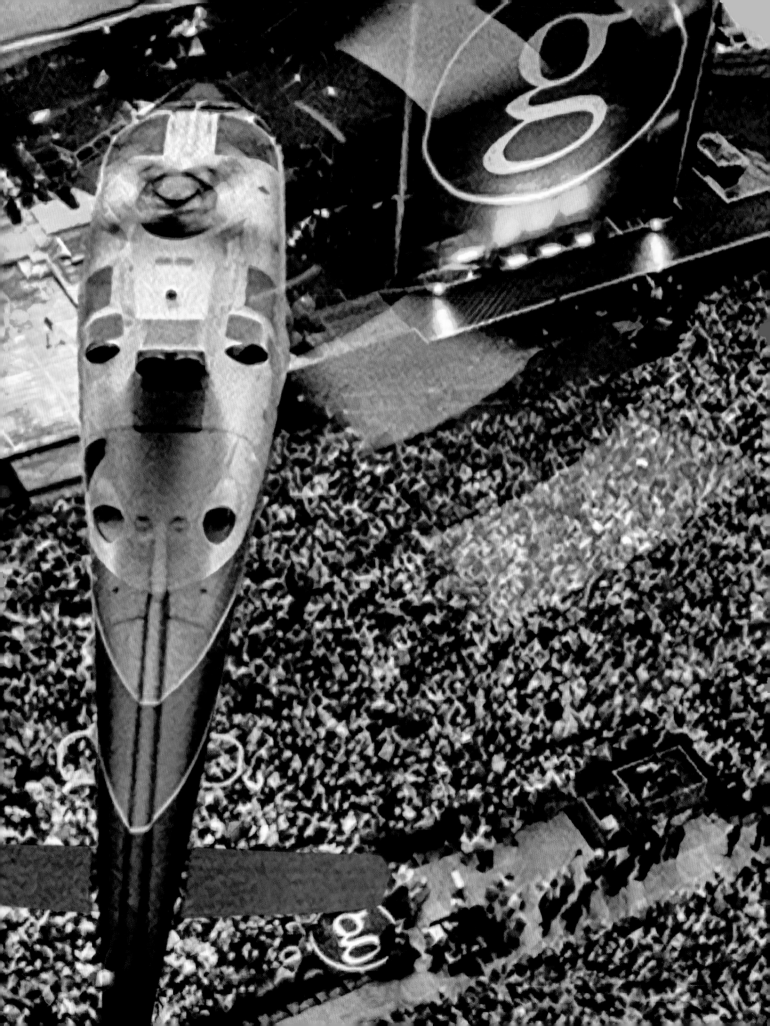

AFTERWORD

The buses rolled away from Texas A&M in late '98, the final gig of the '96-'98 World Tour. It would be the last time Garth would tour for sixteen years.

From the days when Garth Brooks was a college student playing shows in Oklahoma bars to the time he stood in Central Park, playing to more than a million people, and well after, each night Garth Brooks would walk up on a stage to meet his audience. The connection between the people out there and the artist was personal. It was the only way he knew. But behind it all, enjoying one of the most successful careers in the history of popular music, Garth Brooks couldn't stop thinking about the other people in his life who wanted to see him: his children. And while he wasn't the first music-maker to find himself in this predicament, he knew he had to walk away from it all.

For the fans, Brooks' retirement came as a shock. But in some way, watching Brooks step away from his own success to embrace the centerpiece of life, parenting, made him even more believable as a singer, as a performer, as a man in the world. If it's a strong cord connecting the artist to his audience, in that moment it got even stronger. They say absence makes the heart grow fonder. In this case, what would be waiting for Garth when he returned would be bigger than anyone could have ever imagined.

This book was produced by:

MELCHER MEDIA

124 West 13th Street, New York, NY 10011
www.melcher.com

CEO: Charles Melcher
President and CRO: Julia Hawkins
Vice President and COO: Bonnie Eldon
Executive Editor/Producer: Lauren Nathan
Production Director: Susan Lynch
Editor/Producer: Josh Raab
Senior Digital Producer: Shannon Fanuko
Associate Editor/Producer: Karl Daum

Designed by Paul Kepple at Headcase Design, with Chika Azuma

Melcher Media would like to thank Jess Bass, Tova Carlin, Amelie Cherlin, Karl Daum, Sharon Ettinger, Dave Kang, Karolina Manko, Anya Markowitz, Emma McIntosh, Carolyn Merriman, Gabrielle Sirkin, Chris Steighner, Nadia Tahoun, Megan Worman, Avery Quigley, Annika Reff, Katy Yudin, Warren Zanes, and Gabe Zetter.

ACKNOWLEDGMENTS

The Garth Brooks Team would like to thank the following but not limited to: Matt Allen, Kheli Baucom, Nicki Beltranena, Randy Bernard, Anka Brazzell, The Brooks Family, Dallas Cowboys, Don Cobb, Tommy Colorigh, Eric Conn, Tina Crawford, Bob Doyle, Michael Doyle, Andy Friday, Charles Green, Cheryl Harris, Luellyn Latocki Hensley, Dan Johnson, Rusty Jones, Mark Miller, Erika Wollam Nichols, Opry Entertainment, Craig Owens, Jeff Penick, Sam Powers, PRG Lighting, Kevin Pryzbylowski, Steve Puntolillo, Pat Quigley, Allen Reynolds, Nancy Seltzer, Theresa Smith, Virginia Team, Tami Rose Thompson, Trisha Yearwood, and Wendi Crosby York.

… and mostly to God, for it is through Him all things are possible.

PHOTOGRAPHY CREDIT

Nubar Alexanian, Wendy D'Angelo, Henry Diltz, Bob Doyle Collection, Beth Gwinn, Paul House, Alan Mayor, Gary Null and Lewis Lee Courtesy of Production Resource Group, Bev Parker, Vicki Parker, Don Putnam, Sergi Reboredo / Alamy Stock Photo, Maryanne Russell, Michael Schwartz, Tami Rose Thompson, The Tennessean / Part of the USA TODAY NETWORK, and Mick Weber.